Story of the automobile
Its history and development from 1760 to 1917
With an analysis of the standing and prospects of
the automobile industry

H. L. Barber

Alpha Editions

This edition published in 2024

ISBN : 9789362999894

Design and Setting By
Alpha Editions
www.alphaedis.com
Email - info@alphaedis.com

As per information held with us this book is in Public Domain.
This book is a reproduction of an important historical work. Alpha Editions uses the best technology to reproduce historical work in the same manner it was first published to preserve its original nature. Any marks or number seen are left intentionally to preserve its true form.

Contents

PREFACE. ....- 1 -

INTRODUCTION. ....- 5 -

CHAPTER I. INTRODUCTORY—
AUTOMOBILE INDUSTRIAL FIGURES
ARE AMAZING. By Edward G.
Westlake, *Automobile Editor, The Chicago
Evening Post.* ....- 13 -

CHAPTER II. MECHANICAL
EVOLUTION OF THE AUTOMOBILE. ....- 23 -

CHAPTER III. COMMERCIALIZING
THE MOTOR VEHICLE. ....- 39 -

CHAPTER IV. AUTOMOBILE
INDUSTRY AS AN INVESTMENT. ....- 74 -

CHAPTER V. BENEFITS CONFERRED
BY THE AUTOMOBILE. ....- 83 -

CHAPTER VI. REPORT ON
AUTOMOBILES, AUTOMOBILE
ACCESSORIES AND TIRE
MANUFACTURERS' SECURITIES
FROM A FINANCIAL AND
INVESTMENT STANDPOINT.
COMPILED SPECIALLY FOR USE IN THIS

BOOK BY THE BUSINESS BOURSE INTERNATIONAL, INC. NEW YORK CITY. ....- 92 -

CHAPTER VII. PASSENGER AUTOMOBILES MANUFACTURED IN THE UNITED STATES. ....- 125 -

CHAPTER VIII. GASOLINE TRUCKS AND DELIVERY CARS MANUFACTURED IN THE UNITED STATES. .... -138 -

PREFACE.

So far as I know, there is no book in circulation that tells, in concise form, the story of the mechanical and commercial evolution of the automobile, mirrors its sudden leap into popular use, and shows how it has demonstrated, in a most amazing way, the power of money to make money, describes its benefits to the world, and forecasts the future possibilities of the automobile industry as an investment.

This book, the "Story of the Automobile," shows the struggle of man for one hundred and fifty years to devise a means of propelling a vehicle without animal power.

It describes the various stages of the evolution of the idea of motive force other than animal power, in France, England, Germany and the United States, and its triumphant culmination in a successful horseless vehicle. And it makes clear how, when the automobile became of practical use, its successful commercialization became most profitable in the shortest period of time of that of any product of man's ingenuity supplying an article to meet human wants.

But if this were all that could be recorded of the story of the automobile, this book would not have been written. The automobile's success demonstrates all this, and something more—something that would not ordinarily occur to a person unless his attention was called to it.

The astonishing history of the automobile's success affords one of the most convincing and the best modern instance of the opportunities that are being constantly presented for investing for profit.

It is a signal example kept in our hearing every day by the Niagara-like roar of the cars along our boulevards, of the fact that this is the age of golden opportunities for making money make money—of opportunities that disclose themselves, sometimes unexpectedly, and, when embraced, are apt to respond with a veritable avalanche of profits.

For was it not an avalanche of profits that overwhelmed the man who in thirteen years made $200,000,000 and was offered another $200,000,000 for only a small part of his business? And this great fortune made by Henry Ford did not exhaust the Ford automobile's possibilities, for millions are still being taken out of the business, one investor of $2,000 having received over half a million dollars out of it lately.

When men who are not 40 years old today came out of high school they either did not know what an automobile was or, if they had seen one of the very earliest samples, they had no vision of what it would develop into—no conception of what the future had in store for the wabbly horseless vehicle, zig-zagging down the street, as a potential money-maker.

And in the early days of the automobile's struggles for recognition as a promising investment, no banker or other moneyed man could be brought to believe that it held out any reasonable hopes of great gain. No one could foresee, not even the inventors of the automobile, that in less than two decades the business done through its comparative perfection would rank fourth in order of the industries of the United States. And still less was there anybody so foresighted in the possibilities that lie in money to make more money, as to vision the billions of dollars of profits to be paid out by this one idea of a horseless vehicle.

We can find few instances which so forcefully show, as the automobile industry shows, the chances for profitable investment in a short time which may come from sources supplying the needs or pleasures of the great mass of the people.

The chapters of the "Story of the Automobile" devoted to its commercialization make clear that its greatest success has been due to the production of automobiles at a price within reach of people of ordinary means. For this the one man most responsible is Henry Ford. He has demonstrated in a manner of many millions that the most money is to be made out of things used by the greatest number of people—things that become common needs.

The enduring truth of the profitableness of Philip D. Armour's apothegm, "Make and sell things that are 'et' up," is not discredited by the automobile industry, for the use of the automobile "eats" up steel, brass, wood, rubber, leather, gasoline and many other natural resources. The automobile wears out and has to be replaced, so it properly comes in the category of things "et" up.

This truth, that the greatest profits lie in products that can be given general distribution, with a consequent large sale, which is one I have maintained in my book, "Making Money Make Money," in my magazine, "Investing for Profit," and in all my teachings on the science of investing, finds a splendid exemplification in the automobile industry's success as a phenomenally profitable form of investment, and the circumstances of this success are but cumulative evidence of the soundness of my doctrine.

And the success of the automobile industry in the measure and with the speed it has achieved verifies not only this claim I have made and maintained, but confirms my contention of the value of co-operation.

I have preached co-operation as urgently as I have advocated, as the best objects of investment, the value of things used popularly and in quantities.

The "Story of the Automobile" could not have had written into it the glamour of the golden guerdons of Golconda but for Ford's idea of quantity production, reinforced by co-operative standardization of parts. Co-operation between the manufacturers produced standardization, and standardization enabled quantity production, and the low price which quantity consumption warranted has caused automobiles to be bought by millions, and the purchase of the automobile in millions, instead of thousands, has made the hundreds of millions of dividends which this wonderful mine of profits has yielded.

The "Story of the Automobile" is one of the best and most notable proofs of two of my convictions bedded in the concrete of experience, namely, that the most promising investments are those made in natural resources and enterprises which the largest number of people can patronize, and that co-operation is one of the most effective forces in nature, and, therefore, applicable to the affairs of men as a beneficent influence, and, if efficient, the handmaiden of success.

The story of the automobile has herein been treated in a way that not only presents a graphic relation of the automobile's development as an invention, its commercialization, its benefits to man and the position it occupies as a notable example of earning power, but in a manner that develops the many morals taught by its success. The method of treatment of the subject matter is uncommon, and, for this reason, interesting, I trust, to those who read the book.

The chapter contributed by Mr. Edward G. Westlake, automobile editor of the *Chicago Evening Post*, is a resume of automobile conditions from the intimate viewpoint of a writer who has specialized in the automobile, and enjoys a deserved reputation as the dean of the automobile editors of the daily newspaper press. Every one interested in automobiles will derive information and entertainment through reading Mr. Westlake's presentation of the amazing features of automobile industrial figures. In it he states interesting facts not stated elsewhere in the volume.

The book's interest and value as a contribution to automobile literature, of which there is not much in book form, would be less than they are, but for the participation in its preparation by the Business Bourse International,

Inc., New York, whose vice-president, Mr. J. George Frederick, is one of the highest authorities on business economics.

The chapter by the Business Bourse deals with the automobile industry from the standpoint of the financial and investment aspects of the automobile, accessory and tire manufacturers' securities, and Mr. Frederick's reputation in the financial world is a guarantee of the authoritative accuracy of the facts presented in this chapter.

Credit for salient facts in the history of the automobile, obtained and used in the "Story of the Automobile," is given to a large volume of nearly 500 pages, "The Romance of the Automobile Industry," by James Rood Doolittle, issued lately by The Klebold Press, New York city. This volume is the most exhaustive work in book form yet published on the automobile, and covers graphically every phase of its development and popularization. It is virtually a textbook and reference guide of facts of motor car history, and devotes particular attention to the personnel of the founders of the industry and those engaged in it, and the association features.

I can only hope that the work entailed in presenting8 this, the "Story of the Automobile," has been done sufficiently well to make it interesting and instructive to those who read it.

H. L. BARBER.

Wheaton, Ill., April 2, 1917.

INTRODUCTION.

"What did Benjamin Franklin have to do with the automobile?" a great many readers of this book will ask.

Benjamin Franklin was many-sided, and he had a great deal to do with much that affects the birth of the American nation; and if it had not been for what he and other patriots, statesmen and diplomats did, the automobile business might have been in this country today exactly what it is in England today—and that is a very insignificant industry.

Among other things Franklin was a signer of the Declaration of Independence, and it was the American Revolution that made the automobile industry of today possible; for, had there been no revolution, we would probably still be a dominion of Britain beyond the seas, and it is pretty certain that England would have had in force in the colonies the laws she kept on her statute books until 1896, practically prohibiting, by the imposition of excessive road tolls, the use of the public highways to horseless carriages.

For, strange as it may seem to us in this country, which Emerson epitomized as another name for opportunity, the English horse owners and people generally resented, as early as 1840, the progress represented by the automobile, and stifled all development of it from that time to a date when France, Germany and the United States had made it a real factor in transportation.

If, therefore, Franklin had not helped to free this land from the British yoke, the automobile industry might have been in the United States what it is in England today. France and Germany might now have been doing the automobile business of the world, with England and this country buying from them, as England and France are now buying from the United States, whose automobile supremacy at this date is unquestioned.

While the gasoline type of automobile today is the most popular, this is not to say that the electric type is not a success scientifically and commercially. Indeed, the future extent of the automobile's use for commercial purposes is said by experts to depend largely on the electric driven type.

And who will deny that but for Franklin the electric motor would not have been, for it was he who wrested the thunderbolt from heaven, as well as the sceptre of dominion over our land from the tyrant. Franklin as the discoverer of electricity may well be accorded the credit for the electric automobile, which has played no small part in the development of the automobile industry, a fact which every student of automobile history will concede.

It is, however, on an even firmer foundation than either of the causes mentioned that Benjamin Franklin stands as contributing to the success of the automobile industry. The inventors could invent and the manufacturers could make the automobile, but who, pray, was to buy it, if it was to be in general use, if not the common people? And how, may we ask, were the people going to buy it without money?

As the great teacher of frugality and thrift, Franklin laid the cornerstone, 150 years ago, on which the superstructure of the American automobile industry has been erected. For, assuredly, had the seed planted by him failed to germinate and ripen in the American consciousness, we could as well have been today a nation of spendthrifts as a people self-denying, thrifty and frugal. He inculcated those principles of temperance and economy in the lives of our forefathers which have been handed down to us from one generation to another, to our advantage and as an aid to our saving habits, by which we are enabled to buy automobiles.

Many a motor car today owes its ownership to the teachings of Franklin. Many an automobile buyer would never have become one had he not heeded Franklin's injunction, to "Remember, a patch on your coat and money in your pocket is better and more creditable than a writ on your back and no money to take it off," and the investor would not have put money in stocks of automobile companies if he had not learned the truth of Franklin's teaching that "Money makes money, and the money that money makes, makes more money."

Franklin having done what he could to prepare American citizens to economize and save against the day of the automobile, and to invest their money in its manufacture, and the American citizen having followed his teachings and accumulated enough to buy at least a Ford, and perhaps a few shares of automobile company stocks, the man appeared who produced the first gasoline automobile in the United States. That man was Charles E. Duryea. His reputation rests on the fact that, though there were steam and electric automobiles in existence, and the gasoline motor had been developed, he was the first to put gasoline motor and buggy body into co-ordination and make the first run the second. To Duryea, the constructor of the "buggy-aut," is accorded the credit, by automobile history, of being the father of the American gasoline car.

Following Duryea by only one year, came the genius who put into general circulation the universal car.

A reading of Henry Ford's biography discloses that his first idea, that the big money was in production in quantity—that a million articles sold at a profit of 50 cents each was a better paying transaction than ten thousand sold at $3.00 each—was in connection with a watch. Watches and clocks were the first things that Ford subjected to the mechanical promptings of his boyish mind, and he had it all planned out to make a 50-cent watch before Ingersoll had conceived the commercial possibilities of a dollar one.

An accident which his father met with called him from Detroit to the Michigan farm, and this accident deprived the country of a 50-cent watch and gave it a $350 automobile instead. And most people will agree that it was a fair exchange and no robbery. Thomas A. Edison, strange as it may sound, was responsible for the practically universal use of the Ford automobile, for he it was, who, by the chance remark, "What you want to do to make money is to make quantity," started Ford on his downward price career. We have it from Mr. Ford himself that he heard this statement by Edison, and that it so impressed him that he made it the rule and guide of his life; that he never renounced the idea. When, after building a motor that was a success and commanded the attention and capital of moneyed men in Detroit, Ford formed his first company to build his car, this great idea was obstinately adhered to by him, and was the cause of his falling out with his moneyed partners. They could not see the light which has given Ford his halo—the great white light of quantity production. This light burns with steady brilliancy because it is generated by the great principle of the greatest good to the largest number. Ford's associates in his first company were not believers in this principle, evidently, because when they fell out with Ford about it, and Ford got out of the company to start the one he now controls, they went ahead making cars that sell today for from $2,300 to $3,900. But though they have made fair profits, they have not made the fabulous sums that Ford has, and one can only wonder how they feel about it, and if they realize the error of their views. They are probably wiser if not richer.

The success of Ford's idea of quantity sales demonstrates a great fact in the affairs of life. It is that fields of human endeavor are not exhausted or worked out until the human race has ceased to exist. Take any line of enterprise you will, and it has as many facets as a prism. An idea only is needed, which, if the right one, illustrates the enterprise as lights thrown on the prism cause it to sparkle in many colored rays.

We think, for instance, that the acme has been reached in the making and marketing of bread, but along comes a man with an idea for making bread of bran, and he is immediately ushered into the inner sanctum of the temple of great profits. Or we imagine that the last word has been said in cereal foodstuffs, when lo, and behold, the man with the right idea proves that the field has room and to spare for a financial success in so simple a thing as rice dressed in a palatable and salable form. And so it is in everything, automobiles especially. The man who conceives the idea of a sport car supplies a want that others have neglected. There may be many automobile tractors on the market, but the human brain conceives one with some feature lacking in others, such, for instance, as making a Ford automobile interchangeable into a farm tractor, and it has an immediate and large success. And if anybody had an idea that the profits from producing petroleum might be limited by the use of gas and electric light, it was because the automobile's enormous consumption of gasoline and the use of oil by ships could not be foreseen.

The field for investment is kept constantly fallow, and ready for the seed that is to fructify into great profits, by the human brain which is ever active—ever thinking. If its product is not an elemental, it is a supplementary idea, as the rubber tire, the demountable rim and the self-starter for automobiles. Until the world has arrived at perfection in all things, the ultimate will not have been reached. The opportunities of today and tomorrow are as great as they were yesterday. It is a question whether they are not greater, for if the quotation ascribed to Emerson is true, that the world will beat a path to the door, though it be in a forest, of him who makes a mouse trap better than his neighbor, the future possibilities of enterprise are favored by increased population and the element of the cumulative nature of the wants of man. As inventions and articles of use increase in number, new needs which demand supplementary products are created. Each new thing given to the world brings in its train other new things. The crank of a Ford auto creates a demand for a self-starter. The increase in population and wealth brings in its train a multiplication of human units whose use of created things is on a crescendo scale.

The financial successes in the automobile business, great as they are, have followed the inexorable law that the richest returns in all investments are the ground floor ones. The history of no big business demonstrates more clearly that the way to make money is to invest in new companies when they are offering the first authorized capitalization for investment subscription. Money-making opportunities for new investors are always greatest in enterprises whose development is ahead and in the future. If they have reached the stage where development is already producing great profits, the door is closed to the new investor, or else he must pay a premium to sit in such paying company.

In the ground floor days of the Ford money-making machine, Miss Couzens "risked" $100 on Ford. That $100 produced $100,000 in cold cash. But it did so only because the inception of the Ford enterprise provided the opportunity. Having made its half a billion, or more, the Ford enterprise is no longer enterable on any basis that would give such returns for each dollar invested. When money is needed enterprise is willing to pay liberally for its use. When enterprise has all the money it wants, money's value to it is less. This is the most natural law. It is a law that operates in other things besides money. "He that hath, needs not; he that hath not, wants."

The automobile industry illustrates graphically that when an enterprise develops to the point where it is well grounded and has reached a period of age and steady earning capacity, it is not new investors who may come in and gather the richest plums, but the old ones, those who helped to give it its start, who stood by it when the future was obscure, and the ultimate outcome not certain. There is probably no business that shows as many people in it now, who were in it at the start, as the automobile business. This applies to manufacturers, distributors and investors, and is, to a certain extent, due to the industry's newness. The original Ford investors are practically all intact. It is the original investors who have reaped the reward of their courage in embarking in new enterprise, and who have shared in the division of the juicy melons the automobile companies have cut in the form of huge stock and other dividends. We need no better proof of the fact that ground floor investments promise the greatest returns on money invested than the financial history of the automobile.

While quantity production and the co-operative spirit which led to standardization were the keystones in the structure of the present day automobile success, the history of the successful development of the automobile demonstrates another fact, which is a vital one in the realm of investment.

This fact is that most great financial successes are built on our natural resources. This is peculiarly so of the automobile industry. The steel, wood, rubber, leather and glass of which the automobile is composed, are all products of the ground, the forest or the farm. It could not be said that the products of the earth directly make the profits of a stock life insurance company, but this can be said of the automobile industry, and its history discloses that the automobile business of the United States was four times rescued from failure, first, by petroleum, for steam and electric cars would not sell in quantities, and the gasoline from petroleum was needed to give the automobile its great vogue, once by tungsten, vanadium and chromium, again by the quantity production theory, and finally by co-operative standardization.

At one period of automobile development, the manufacturers were ready to give up in despair because cold-rolled and high carbon steels only were available, and these made the weight of the car and the price obstacles to its popular adoption. At the stage when failure to produce a car at popular price was imminent, there entered on the scene tungsten, chromium, vanadium and aluminum, all natural resources, and they, combining with standardization, made quantity production possible. Tungsten, alloyed with steel for valves, chrome steel for springs, vanadium in steel to impart purity, and aluminum for lightness, reduced the weight of the automobile 25 per cent, enabled motors to be made smaller, tires lighter, original cost less, and cut down upkeep cost to the users of cars. Quantity production thus was made possible, and natural resources again vindicated their claim to being premier possibilities of profit.

Of the future of the automobile and of products allied with it or sharing in its construction and prosperity, as continuing money-makers, all indications are that the profits already taken out of the motor car industry in the United States are but placer croppings, and that the years to come will record the workings of the real vein. This real vein, in the opinion of the man who looks ahead, is in the use of passenger cars, haulage trucks and motor tractors by the fifty million of the population of this union of states who are on or of the farm.

As yet, the farmers have not risen to the full possibilities of motor power in economic superiority over horse power for haulage, ground cultivation, and other uses to which the horse is now put. Elements which will hasten this awakening are the scarcity of man labor and the workings of the immutable law of economics. There is not enough food being produced by the world to supply the demand. If there were, prices would be lower. Prices will remain high as long as the supply falls below the demand. As long as they remain high, the stimulation to greater production will continue, and this urge can have but one result, which is to force the producer to adopt the most economical method of production.

It has been determined that motor power is cheaper than horse power. It is, therefore, only a question of time when the horse will go from the farm as he is disappearing from the cities. In this evolution will be found the money-making possibilities of investment in the motor tractor and the motor truck. Their adaptation to the smallest as well as the largest needs of the tiller of the land is now being assured.

With the horse, the farmers of the United States have been able to break up only 70 per cent of the cultivable land not in timber. There are over two hundred million acres of tillable land that have never felt the cold steel of a chilled plow. There are two hundred million more acres in timber that will, much of it, ultimately come under the plow. Besides crippling the labor supply in this country, the European war has taken a million horses out of our supply. The case in favor of the tractor coming ultimately into common use seems from all this to be completely made out—its adoption in large numbers being only a question of getting the price down to a basis which will insure quantity production. As this was done with passenger automobiles, it would be folly to say it will not be done with tractors and trucks.

Figures showing the total amount of money that has been taken in profits out of the automobile industry have never been compiled. It is a business that has developed so rapidly and feverishly that the water churned up by the commotion it has made has not yet settled. But there is a record of enough individual instances of gigantic profits to prove that the largest individual appetite for dividends should have been satisfied by the ratio of earnings already made in automobile manufacture.

But in every case the greatest profits were in the stock of those companies that complied with Edison's rule of large money-making—"What you want to do to make money is to make quantity." And they were also companies which made an automobile that could be "'et' up," as Armour put it, by time and use, in less time than it takes time and use to eat up a higher priced machine.

Ford, Overland, Reo—you will recognize this trinity as the leaders in sales, and by the same token they have been the leaders in profits. When it is stated that Henry Ford made $200,000,000 in thirteen years, and was then offered a like amount for only a small part of his enterprise, we may well believe that he credits his own statement that "anything for only a few people is no good. It's got to be good for everybody or it won't survive." Other Ford investors profited on the basis of $5,000,000 for each $10,000 invested. After the parent Ford company had established a record of a million dollars a week in profits in the United States alone, Ford stepped across the river into Canada and organized a company there which is earning fifty per cent a year on its capital of $10,000,000.

Profits of $52,000,000 in capital stock alone which has been built up almost entirely of dividends earned, is the record of the Willys-Overland Company. John North Willys founded the success of this great money-making business on his personal check of $500, cashed at great trouble during the panic of 1907, when the Overland company was ready to go into bankruptcy. Besides the dividends applied to increasing the capital, an immense amount in profits has been disbursed by this enterprise. The dividends in 1916 were $11,000,000, over 20 per cent of the capital. This year they will likely be nearly double that amount. The Reo Motor Car Company has paid over $50,000 on an investment of $1,000. These three are not by any means all the automobile companies which have contributed to make the automobile industry a signal example of the earning power of money, but they represent the leaders of the popular or quantity-production-through-low-price type. There are about 150 passenger automobile companies that are profitable in varying degrees, proportioned to their price, not to say anything of trucks and tractors, in the marketing of which fortunes are also being made.

CHAPTER I.

INTRODUCTORY—AUTOMOBILE INDUSTRIAL FIGURES ARE AMAZING.
By Edward G. Westlake,
Automobile Editor, The Chicago Evening Post.

During the year 1916 the automobile industry in the United States entered the "billion dollar class," and manufacturers who have membership in the National Automobile Chamber of Commerce which holds the industry, as it were, in the hollow of its great hand, made no more ado over this significant, almost amazing development than to meet in the annual banquet and reiterate their statements that the critic did not live who could predict, with certainty, the gain that might be made in 1917.

It was expected that the industry would climb into the billion dollar fold—men said that the fourth industry in the country had the financial stage set for starring the "Big Billion," and they never permit themselves to see a possibility of a recession unless steel becomes too great to be kept within bounds—in short material price is the only problem the venturesome automobile maker will put down for earnest discussion.

Accurate figures spread on the records of the National Automobile Chamber of Commerce indicate that retail sales of motor vehicles in 1916 totaled $1,068,028,273. This total includes a production of 1,525,578 cars and 92,130 trucks. The passenger cars were valued at $921,378,000 and the trucks were listed at $166,650,275. When the statisticians of the national organization compared figures and found the gain was 80 per cent, and paused long enough to find that the gain the year previous had been 36 per cent, they talked about the complete automobilization of the country and the inevitable addition of more than 2,000,000 to the total of cars in operation in the United States.

PRICE DROP IN ONE YEAR.

Weight decreased, as the engineers had planned, and the average price of cars decreased in one year from $671 to $605. In the eight previous years the average price of automobiles had dropped from $2,125 to $814. Wall Street, which once had only the cold shoulder for the automobile producer, took a permanent seat at the table where daily the industry was dissected, analyzed, weighed, discussed and reviewed; and, as a result, it is as difficult to keep from the financial eyes of Wall Street the operations of the great automobile factories as it would be to hide the clearing house reports. The keenest financial and commercial experts of the United States have learned to keep the motor car industry constantly under surveillance—not that they mistrust the manufacturers, but that they have found the industrial situation is so firmly linked to the dollars and cents program of the country's economy that nothing may successfully act to deprecate the importance of the auto industry. Time was when General Motors sold as low as 40—what Stock Exchange expert would expect to see this stock sell for less than 105?—and if conditions were to become so chaotic that General Motors, with its prosperous units, were to break to a point or two under par, what financial student would not search for something akin to a Black Friday?

Immutable laws work in the automobile industry. The maker daily takes a course in the University of Production, because an army of selling factors constantly is attending to the absorption facilities of the country's markets and he rarely permits himself the task of figuring on the "probable saturation point." It is a wonderfully important thing to the maker that the national Organization gets official reports, guides the policies of standardization, holds an indefinable influence over the engineers of the industry, and sits as the congress of the Republic of Motor Car Production. The auto industry of today is, perhaps, the most intricate thing in the country, and yet so responsive to the law of supply and demand that there is not an element of guesswork in it.

Although more than two hundred automobile concerns that had entered the arena of business, developing from the "blue print stage" to manufacturing concerns of considerable output, had failed in the last twelve years, the automobile industry had been a big paying one. Pioneers who remain and whose works annually pay dividends, accepted the failures as the necessary concomitant of a great business that only showed an output of 3,700 cars in 1899 and only 11,000 vehicles in 1903, the amount growing to 485,000 cars in the year 1913.

"Our house is a generally well ordered one," the maker delighted in saying. "The industry is like a science. The engineer has brought standardization to almost finality, the matter of styles and body designs is an exact science, the tire companies have been keen rivals but beneath their terrific competition they have permitted the stream of co-operation in tire standardization to run smoothly, and the manufacturer has spent his money wisely in equipping his plant with plenty of large-quantity type of machinery and increased his plant to enable him to handle the large production. Increased production in economically managed plants spells the maximum of profit."

POINT OF SATURATION FAR OFF.

And with experts bold enough to say that the field of prospects facing the industry numbers 5,000,000 probable buyers, little thought is given to imminence of "saturation" and a consequent rehabilitation of the motor manufacturing and distributing plans. In the plainest language that it is possible for the automobile maker to use he says today: "The maker who has an adequate organization and builds a pleasure car or truck that is as good as specified and who permits no retrogression in his organization, will succeed."

"Luxury and necessity." The automobile maker is willing to have his product classed in this way. For the early years of the industry the car was a clear cut "luxury." It weighed so much that its cost was prohibitive to the big family of "Necessity." The car simply had to be "had" by men of large incomes. Automobiles were not sold by intensive salesmen in those days—the family bought them, even as a fine jewel was purchased at the great jewelry houses. Tremendous prices were paid, in comparison to the set prices of the automobile industry at this day. The "make" of the car that stood in front of the owner's home often was accepted as a basis for rating the social position of the owner. Seat cushions, slip covers, fine upholstery and the name plate on the car told a big and varied story.

Immediately following the craze to buy the high priced cars, developed the "man Friday" of the industry—the chauffeur. And the chauffeur worked readily with the wealthy man, often advising the purchase of the foreign machine upon which Uncle Sam collected a very large duty. But the foreign made car had its stamp of distinction, perhaps much easier to utilize in the form of extravagant, even snobbish, style of life that the owner of the foreign car elected to affect, and the United States manufacturer of cars was not at all prepared to put out a car that would correct the desire of Americans to drive around in an imported article.

But the domestic car had a friend in this contingency. Economical living was that friend. Ruin often followed the extravagance of those who bought the high priced and, as many experts said, inferior imported cars. Homes were mortgaged and all the financial trails were traversed in the effort to maintain an impossible extravagant life. The banker began to detest the automobile. It seemed to him that it was undermining the life of the nation. Something had to be done to correct, also, the tone of the domestic automobile maker's life. He developed a desire for watered stock. Over capitalization of his plant was suspected by the banking interests, and on every hand the motor car industry was decried. Waste and inflation stalked arm in arm through many plants. It even was said that the industry was only a "game"; that incompetent executives kept their eyes on the broker's tape, while corps of associates in the factories were ready to play the "game" for all it would stand.

Few were blind to the prospects in the motor industry at that time, if the financial interests of the country were estranged; but no one was able to withstand the developments. The fire of criticism cleaned out the dross. Organization, the big thing needed to eliminate the "game" and give the industry the foundation upon which the large "billion dollar business" subsequently was built, began to come into being. Men of energy and brains got to work. These characters have remained. There are those veterans of the industry who say that the year 1907 marked the start of the business on the basis of a real industry. In that year 44,000 cars was the total output, and the value of the product was registered at $93,400,000. This was the highest total of value for the output of the industry so far reached in the United States.

The next year the industry built 85,000 cars, valued at $137,800,000, and quantity production, efficient buying of material, strict attention to cost production in the plants, effective steps toward standardization, engineering methods that abolished a great deal of weight, etc., began to be set standards among car makers. The official statements of the industry show how well the improvements fitted in. In 1909 the production of automobiles amounted to 126,500, valued at $164,200,000. The following year the output climbed above the 200,000 mark, and since then the production figures have mounted steadily. Automobiles were *sold* and competition became keener, but the output increased.

VALUE OF RELIABILITY CONTESTS.

With the new era of development in the early nineties came into prominence farseeing manufacturers who paid heed to the thought that the best way to put a fit and efficient motor car into the hands of the public was to test the car, its material and its mechanical practices, in some officially conducted series of reliability contests. Besides, it was urged there was a "romance of business" attached to the motor car industry that would lead to a greatly increased amount of publicity in the press.

The national annual reliability competitions grew into wonderful favor. Makers strove hard to win the reliability titles. The "Glidden" tours became the tests that attracted not only the attention of every automobile man, but the general public. The whole country became the testing ground. For several years these national events did well the work they were expected to perform. Automobile building received, perhaps, its most practical aid. Makers learned. They took advantage both of the mechanical data and the publicity. A complex but valuable adjunct of the national tours became popular—every region in which the American Automobile Association was a factor, and this organization continues to be a powerful aid to the industry, had its reliability or its endurance classic.

It has been said that the manufacturers of automobiles lost interest in national reliability tours after the test of 1911. Perhaps many did. But the truth, as told by a wonderfully efficient engineer, is that there remained nothing more that a national tour could teach the car builder. He had measured the power of his steel to withstand shock, he had calculated the efficiency of his motor to stand its daily tasks on a strenuous schedule, he had learned of the troubles of his rivals and he had spent his money liberally, at the direction of his engineering department, to make a car that would do anything a less skillful driver than a national tour pilot could ask of the machine. The national tour became a luxury. It was revived in 1913 on the long and strenuous grind from Minneapolis to the Rocky Mountains, and an immense amount of valuable information was the result. But the national tour seems to be now chiefly remembered by the occasional discourse of an engineer who tells of the long struggles in the mud and the hardships of sand and dust storms.

With the added development of the plants, came another reason why the national tour was not necessary. Testing tracks were added to the maker's plant assets. Testing on the roads followed the block tests of the motors, and it began to be accepted as an axiom in the industry that the engineer knew to a hair's breadth what his engine could do before it went out of the secret room where the chief engineer worked.

Meanwhile prices constantly were beaten down. The field of opportunity to own a car widened. It was, even then, so much bigger, in comparison to that in the Old World, that even the clerk and small salaried man in general looked with a smile toward the day when he would own a car.

It is recalled that when the manufacturer began boldly to put the farmer in the class of available prospects—openly declared his idea of building a car that he could sell in the agricultural districts as readily as cars were sold in the city districts, one man who this year is making 750,000 automobiles, gave to the world his edict which resulted later in the United States court sustaining his contention that the "Selden patent" under which the organization of makers was maintaining its official life, "was not basic, in fact was not worth the paper it was printed on," and he would refuse ever to recognize the right of the national organization to grant licenses to make the internal combustion engine and the chassis that went with it.

The public read with a strange feeling, the record of the great litigation against the "basic patent." It seemed like a battle of Titans, and ordinary folk thought it might result in danger to the industry. But only the lawyers were strenuously engaged. They argued and submitted briefs for more than two years, the national organization of the makers who accepted the license of the "Selden patent," honoring their national organization by paying to the treasury their pro rata on the amount of cars made.

An enormous fund grew. But the man who wanted to make from 200,000 to 750,000 cars a year was determined. He won in the Federal court and almost immediately the "licensed association" began to break up. The contributions of license fees ceased and soon the association was a thing of history. It was succeeded by the National Chamber of Commerce which has become the senate, house of congress—the parliament, if you please— of the automobile industry in the United States. Some, there were, who had a very poorly defined idea of the actual mission of the "licensed association," believing that it was a "trust," called its function destructive. They thought that the officers of the association would lay an embargo upon certain manufacturers and allot a more liberal figure on annual output to the larger and stronger firms in the organization.

Ford, a "Wizard" and "Genius."

Unfortunately at that time, the licensed association had not the grasp on patent protective measures, engineering work, standardization, etc., that obtains in the present national organization, and the real mission of the licensed association never became wholly evident to the public. But the organization did its part in laying the foundations of the industry. It made the handwriting on the wall for popular price so large, that every man who subsequently invested a dollar in automobile making read, pondered and agreed. It placed popular price and standardization of mechanism in the same category—linked them so that the words of the Detroit automobile manufacturing wizard became axioms. The Detroit genius had proved that the depth and capacity of the automobile market was exactly in ratio to the possible price reduction. Amazing but true, the big men said, was the field that the lower priced car opened to the thoughtful maker of cars. Manufacturers began to talk of some day building and selling as high as a million automobiles in one year. Others calmly declared that when the motor car sales in cities began to "slow up," there would be still more than 5,000,000 prospects in the agricultural districts. Others drew diagrams intended to show that there would be a market for any priced cars that were built in this country, the few persons with large incomes assimilating all the high priced cars, and the many with average incomes absorbing the quantity production at popular prices. All allowances were made for the increase in the cost of labor, materials such as steels and other metals, leather, etc., and some even went far enough to include the possibility of a foreign war on large proportions and its effect upon the industry.

No one gave concrete thought at that time to the possibility of a skillfully conducted partial payment organization of a national nature that would aid the small salaried man in buying his automobile on time payments. But that came about and still is working out its part in the great economic scheme of distribution of the factory output. The makers did not essay digging into the dealers' and distributors' plans for moving cars delivered to them for cash from the factories, and they were not bold enough to say they could finance any time payment and chattel mortgage plans. But many of them admitted the great value of the plan, if a distributer, through a proper alliance with his banker, could make sales in that manner and realize his money. The public learned well, early, that the maker of cars rarely consigned any automobiles to a dealer. The maker sold for cash—the draft had to be presented by the dealer or distributer before he could unload the freight car. It would be legitimate business, the public said, for any automobile dealer to finance himself so that he could sell cars on time. On time today is a mighty big phrase in the industry. It means many a car added to the annual output.

With the growth of incomes in the United States the statisticians found there were more than 6,000,000 people in this country with annual incomes of more than $1,200, and 3,500,000 with annual incomes of more than $1,800. All these things aided in installing confidence in the big men of the motor industry. Quantity production became the password for the manufacturer. A new development in distribution was wonderfully improved—dealers from all over the country were brought to the factory of the car maker, and after a convention of a few days, the dealers were invited to sign up for the coming year, nominating the number and type of models they would buy. The maker pored over his order blanks when the dealers left, made his plans for material accordingly, and there was only prosperity in each automobile factory, as a rule, for the remainder of the year. The orders were indicative of, safely speaking, sixty per cent of the signed total. Some makers took chances and built very close to the total agreed on by the dealers, and, except in few cases, the scheme worked out. Today the maker studies all conditions and accepts the orders of his dealers, setting the figure of output after numerous factory conferences.

Makers who could point to an annual production of, say 400 cars, took counsel among themselves, and some 50 increased their factory efficiency and financial responsibility that they can now point to an output of as many cars in one day as they made early in their manufacturing experience in one season.

The writer recalls one manufacturer who, about nine years ago, had an output of about 500 cars for one season. Only recently he paid close to a quarter of a million dollars, if indeed his extra expenses did not bring the total to $300,000, to conduct a twenty-one day convention at his factory covering a site of seventy-nine acres, at which dealers from the four quarters of the country were entertained. He had daily meetings in the big halls of his administration building, and his lieutenants carefully outlined to all the plans of the company for the year, and exploited the line of models.

"We have $30,000,000 in materials purchased, and expect to get all this material when we need it for manufacturing cars," said the big man to his dealers. "But the war in Europe has caused many problems of price and quantify to arise, and heaven only knows what the material situation will be after July 1. I advise you to order all the cars you need—think well of your requirements—and stick by that number. Then you will not be like many are bound to be, who are indifferent to manufacturing conditions—you will have cars to meet the biggest demand the industry ever has known."

That automobile president had the pleasure of meeting thousands of dealers, speaking to more than one thousand of them daily, and with his factory production manager he figured the probable needs of his country-wide organization of dealers and branch houses for the year. It is significant that the few changes he made on his early winter production table, which the writer was permitted to scan, were made only in the "increase columns."

THE PART MACHINING PLAYS.

It would lead to the exhaustion of the reader were many details to be given showing how the makers made quantity production and economy of factory operation an assured thing. The largest rooms of wholly automatic machinery were equipped, so that a large amount of crude steel wires, rods, etc., practically go into a factory at one end and come out at the other, fully machined and ready to go into the assembly of a machine. Cylinder boring, all with one operation, takes the place of operations that required many hours. Progressive types of assembly of the finished components of the cars make factories look like the "last words in manufacturing." Machining crankcases and work of that nature that required hours, is done in minutes. Aluminum, that magic metal of the early days of the automobile industry, when it was comparatively cheap, now enters so largely into engine and other parts that at its greatly increased price it is more than a magic metal. It is no uncommon thing to find in an automobile factory that a machine costing more than one hundred times the maker's cost of an automobile, has been installed to hasten production.

In all the field of manufacturing there has not been wrought such magic as in gear cutting. Forges pound out tons of steel forms, but the most important machinery of a plant soon has these forms turned into gears and other machined parts for the assembly.

The medium priced car of today stands as the best exemplification of the approval of the Society of Automobile Engineers. This is an organization that has done so much for the manufacturer that most of the makers of cars are members. They point to the self-starter and the electric lighted car as the triumph of the Society of Automobile Engineers. And certainly from the original starter and the early lighting effects, enormous strides have been made in the industry. Fully equipped cars predominate now, where only a few years ago even tops were not provided with the car as sold on the floor.

The self-starter is considered one of the greatest of the improvements added to a good automobile. With this feature the car has become so useful to women that the manufacturers have realized big returns. Better than that, say some critics, is the verdict that the self-starter returned—the chauffeur is no longer an indispensible feature in car driving. Women master the handling of a car and with the machines requiring less mechanical attention, one might say, every season, woman accepts the gasoline car as her own. The number of women drivers has grown so wonderfully that the makers of cars have registered the woman driver as a constant factor. There's no cranking of the car necessary, and the wearing of fine raiment and white shoes is Milady's prerogative, even if she drives her car to the party herself. She handles a multi-cylinder car quite as readily and with the confidence of a man. The tires, always a problem, have demountable rims, or they may be set in spare wire wheels, and troubles on the road from blowouts and punctures no longer deter the woman driver. It would be difficult to get the details on the number of women drivers added to the list each season, but one of the best known automobile makers says that it is so large that he would make his fortune safe if he only made cars henceforth for women pilots. The entrance of the woman in such an important manner in the automobile driving situation has made the gas car maker lose all fear of the greater development of the electric car. Woman has played an important part in the real estate world, distinctly due to her eagerness to drive cars, by starting a movement towards suburbs. The suburbs are "farther out and yet closer" as one maker put it.

Good Roads Industry's Greatest Aid.

When the full effect of the work of good roads advocates is felt in this country, and regular appropriations are to be available in a regularly scheduled manner in most of the states, the biggest thing the automobile industry ever had to help it will have taken up its task in earnest. Less than ten per cent of the roads in this country are improved, say the good roads statisticians. One says that at least two-thirds of the reasons for present road developments are automobile reasons. When the proportion rises and the Lincoln Highway and scores of other long distance highways, intended to add to the cross country touring practice, are made into complete roads that make for genuine touring pleasure, the automobile industry will reap great benefits—more than the most enthusiastic ever dreamed would come from concrete, brick and other forms of specially prepared highways.

The war? Makers have varied opinions on the effect of the termination of the war in Europe. A majority have expressed the opinion that our exports of trucks and pleasure cars will take a big jump soon after peace is declared. But seeking for a peace after the years of warfare has become the least of the American auto maker's trouble. Great war orders have been received and filled by the American makers of trucks. In 1914-15 the war orders rose to 14,000 trucks, as compared with only 784 in the season 1913-14. War orders still are being filled by some American truck makers, or were until the "ruthless submarine warfare" broke out anew, and after millions of dollars worth of the old models bought up in the United States and absorbed by the European powers had been swallowed in the mystery of the continent, United States truck makers began on later design models. In that way they are able to admit that the war has been a great blessing to the motor truck feature of the industry. "All a part of the great scheme of economics that makes for the approach of the complete automobilization of the country," is the way one manufacturer puts it.

The automobile industry is set—it is fourth in importance in the United States. It will handle itself, so to speak. The makers know they must give value for every car and truck they build, and the people have become ready to continue in the industry every maker who plays the industry as it should be—not as a "game."

CHAPTER II.

MECHANICAL EVOLUTION OF THE AUTOMOBILE.

The history of every advance toward greater perfection in the achievements of mankind, whether moral or physical, has been one of slow and laborious development.

We speak carelessly of the wonderful advance the automobile has made in a short time.

As a matter of fact, it has taken the automobile a hundred and fifty years to arrive mechanically at the point it has reached today.

We thought the development of the motor car was speedy, but we find that the measure of time required for its evolution, when put beside the span of human history, lengthens as the shadows grow longer in the dying day.

It is astonishing what stages this development has had to pass through, what problems have confronted it, and what apparently insuperable obstacles it has had to overcome.

In the light which our knowledge of the automobile now sheds on the present day mechanism of this invention, it is difficult for us to realize why these persistent struggles toward development of the mechanical ideas summoned to the aid of the inventors did not produce speedier results.

We can hardly conceive as we look upon the perfect limousine, skimming over the smooth asphalt with a motion that contains no more vibration than that in the glide of the expert ice skater, the crudeness, cumbersomeness and racking joltiness of its first forbear, which was the original expression of the mechanical idea involved in making wheels revolve by a motive power other than that exercised by man, the bullock or the horse.

If we want to relieve our minds of the strain of comprehending the difference between the automobile de luxe, as we of today know it, and the first automobile ever produced, and, by putting the two pictures side by side, span the period of the development of the art of automobile making, we must journey to Paris.

For, although internal combustion to drive a piston in a cylinder was produced with gun-powder in 1678 by Abbe D'Hautefeuille, and a carriage to be driven without the horse was a chaise propelled by human foot work, first conceived by John Vevers of England in 1769, there is no record that the two ideas were combined until it was done in France somewhere between 1760 and 1770.

The first automobile ever made was that produced by Nicholas Joseph Cugnot, a Frenchman, and it is today on exhibition in the Conservatory of Arts and Trades in Paris.

There is no record of how Cugnot came to conceive the idea of his invention, but it is surmised that he had read about James Watt, in England, having discovered the principle of steam as motive power. This was about 1755.

The history of Watt's experiments in applying steam to run engines does not, however, disclose that any engines he produced were ever seen by Cugnot, or that any adequate description of them was published at the time when Cugnot could have taken advantage of it.

So all we may actually know of Cugnot's reasons for thinking he could make an "animalless" road vehicle is locked up in the rickety century-and-a-half-old Cugnot invention which we may see in the Paris Conservatory.

And what we would see would be:

An object which might make us laugh, did we not soberly reflect, in the light of our superior knowledge of today, that it was the first step in the long, laborious journey, extending over 157 years, that inventors had to travel to produce our luxurious limousine, our satisfying touring car and our terrifying speed demon of the oval racing course.

Cugnot's body returned to dust 113 years ago, but his idea went marching on.

The visible expression of this idea which we can see in the Paris Conservatory is in the form of a tractor for a field gun, Cugnot having been a captain in the engineering corps of the French army.

The tractor has a single drive wheel actuated by two single acting brass cylinders, connected by an iron steam pipe with a round boiler of copper containing fire pot and chimneys.

Attached to this first motor-driven road vehicle is a wagon, on which it was Cugnot'a idea to have a field gun mounted.

On either side of the single drive wheel of this clumsy contrivance are located ratchet wheels. Pistons acting alternately on these ratchet wheels revolved the drive wheel in quarter revolutions.

For the copper boiler of this first motor car, additional water was needed after the machine had travelled a few feet, the exhaust of steam quickly leaving the boiler dry. The speed attained was very slow, by reason of the mechanical complications in transmitting power to the drive wheel. As for running smoothly, the machine wobbled, and bumped, and strained, and groaned, and finally ran into a wall. This was because it was overbalanced by its boiler and engine and had no steering gear.

Having run into a wall and been partially wrecked, that was the end of the forerunner of the automobile, except for its subsequent rescue from a junk heap and its installation in the Paris Conservatory; for, disheartened by what he regarded as his failure to make a successful steam-driven tractor to relieve men and other animals of the burden of transporting field guns, Cugnot turned his attention to devising a cavalry gun, at which he was so successful that when he died in 1804 he was enjoying a pension of 1,000 livres a year, given him by Napoleon.

Cugnot could not, of course, have visioned what his first crude automobile would develop into in the next century and a half. He probably never thought of a car holding seven passengers—much less of a speed for it of 60 miles an hour and more. In truth, since he abandoned his efforts, he probably concluded the obstacles in the way of even a practical fulfillment of his idea were insurmountable.

The one fact remains to keep company with the Cugnot motor tractor in the Conservatory of Paris, that Cugnot was the father of the idea out of which the automobile was evolved. He was the first to invent a motor-driven road vehicle.

English Make Automobiles Almost Practicable.

THE ENGLISH PEOPLE HAVE AN ENVIABLE RECORD FOR SUCCESSFUL MECHANICAL INVENTIONS, AND THEY WERE EARLY EXPERIMENTERS ON LINES SIMILAR TO THOSE OF CUGNOT. ABOUT THE TIME THAT CUGNOT RAN HIS MACHINE INTO A WALL, WILLIAM MURDOCK, A MECHANIC, WAS WORKING FOR WATT, THE ENGLISH INVENTOR OF STEAM. WHETHER HE KNEW OF CUGNOT'S AUTOMOBILE ATTEMPT OR NOT, THERE IS NO EVIDENCE EXTANT. THE IDEA OF AN ENGINE-RUN ROAD CONTRIVANCE MAY HAVE COME TO HIM THROUGH INSPIRATION, OR IN SOME OTHER WAY, AS IT DID TO CUGNOT.

MURDOCK WAS QUITE FAMILIAR WITH WATT'S ENGINES. HE HELPED TO BUILD THEM, AND HE WAS CURIOUS TO KNOW THE DIFFERENT FORMS IN WHICH THEY COULD BE USED, ESPECIALLY AS TO A ROAD VEHICLE. HE TALKED TO WATT, BUT WAS STERNLY DISCOURAGED BY THE LATTER. JUST AS CUGNOT, NO DOUBT, CONCLUDED THAT HIS AUTOMOBILE WOULD NEVER GET ANYWHERE, WATT OPPOSED APPLYING HIS ENGINE TO A ROAD TRAVELLING MACHINE, BECAUSE HE WAS FIRMLY convinced that no vehicle that could be invented could successfully negotiate, at a speed to make it worth while, the execrable roads of that day.

In this we have a fine illustration of the peculiarities and uncertain nature of the human mind. It is an organism that astounds by its perception of possibilities in one direction, while numb of any sensation whatever in glimpsing the possibilities in another direction.

Watt could invent steam, but he could not imagine good roads. Had he possessed the vision, he might have seen that roads, which he so abhorred as to see nothing good in them, would be reformed if he but encouraged applying his engines to road travelling mechanism.

In William Murdock's way of taking the doleful discouragement of Watt, we see an illustration of that mental attitude that man has universally adopted in mechanical advance, toward the lugubrious prophet of failure. He has matched hope and optimism against despair and pessimism.

Despite Watt and his mournful views of the impossibility of building an engine-run road carriage that would advance over English roads, Murdock went ahead and built a model of an engine-run road carriage; but when he had it finished, Watt's discouraging views prevailed, and Murdock did not attempt to enlarge his model to a full sized form. He stopped with the model, which is at the present day in the British Museum.

Murdock's invention was tested, and the tests showed that an advance in efficiency over the creation of Cugnot had been made. The model was driven by a single cylinder of three inch bore. It had a one and a half inch stroke. A crank converted the reciprocating motion of the steam engine into rotary motion, the service performed in the Cugnot invention by the quarter revolution ratchet drive. Murdock's idea was patented by a man named Pickard, in 1780.

The first automobile known to have been constructed and put on the road was built by Richard Trevithick at Camborne, England, in 1801. It was in the form of a stage coach, accommodating six or seven persons. The engine, boiler and firebox were at the rear. The engine was one of the first high pressure engines. A single cylinder motor was employed, and spur gear and crank axle were used to transmit the motion of the piston rod to the drive wheels.

With this coach Trevithick carried six or seven men over hills for a mile the first day of the trial. The second day it made six miles. Even with these performances, the invention's impracticability must have been decreed, because it was not continued in operation.

Trevithick himself felt, no doubt, that it must be improved upon, for, in 1803, he built another contrivance driven by a horizontal single cylinder with 5½-inch bore and a 30-inch stroke. But the driving wheels were ten feet in diameter. Fatal were these great clumsy wheels to popular approval of the invention, and no further advance was made. Trevithick had made one further step, and there the matter rested. He had developed the high pressure steam engine, and he had really made the first automobile, if such it could be called.

America's Early Efforts in Automobile Making.

Just as the English, represented by Murdock and Trevithick, were laboring on the steam propulsion idea, and France, in the person of Cugnot, was experimenting with it, so America was groping to find the solution. Cugnot's activities began about 1760 and ended with his death in 1804. Trevithick's period was from 1780 to 1803. The American experiments started about 1784. The man whom records show to have been the pioneer in practical excursions into the realm of carriages driven by steam, was Oliver Evans, born in Delaware but living in Philadelphia.

He developed the high pressure, non-condensing engine, although his only knowledge of steam was derived from reading what little was then printed about it, and his own discoveries. It appears as if Evans, who is known to have had knowledge of Cugnot's construction of a road carriage, or, more properly speaking, a gun carriage, connected in his mind his engine with a road travelling vehicle, because in 1787, four years before Trevithick built his steam coach at Camborne, England, Evans secured a patent from the State of Maryland, giving him the exclusive right to make and use, within its borders, carriages propelled by steam.

That he immediately built a steam carriage in pursuance of this authority is doubtful. The only authentic record of an attempt is of one that he constructed in Philadelphia seven years later and under peculiar circumstances. It is likely that his act in securing the Maryland patent was done on the spur of a determination to build an automobile, but it was not immediately carried out. He went on perfecting steam engines up to 1804, when he accepted an order from the city of Philadelphia to build a steam flat boat for dock work.

His mind appears to have then reverted back to the time seven years before when he contemplated applying an engine to a road vehicle and got the Maryland patent for that purpose, for, after building the steam flatboat and installing a 5-horse power engine on it, he announced his intention of mounting the flatboat on a wagon, on which he proposed to drive the boat about Philadelphia.

A horseless carriage, no doubt, had been a hobby with him for years, and he saw in the steam driven wagon, carrying a steam driven flatboat, an ocular demonstration of the practicability of the horseless carriage.

The four wheels of the wagon he built were connected by belts and gearing with the engine on the boat, and the vehicle was driven up Market Street by steam, bearing the flatboat and its engine in triumph. It circled the squares on which the City Hall and the statue of William Penn now stand, and proceeded to the Schuylkill river. Here flatboat and wagon were separated, and the former launched on the river. A paddle wheel was affixed to the stern and connected with the engine. The boat ran as well as the wagon had done. It steamed down to the Delaware river and all the way to Trenton. The wagon, divorced of engine and gearing, became only a wagon again, and whatever became of it, history does not say.

The skepticism, the derogatory observations, the pessimistic prophecies and the contemptuous disapproval of the many persons witnessing the Evans' pilgrim's progress up Market Street aroused the inventor's ire.

Had he but been philosophical, he would have appreciated that such has been the fate and greeting of all inventions. But Evans was choleric. When a citizen said his wagon was only what might now be dubbed a "flivver"—that it would never run over five miles an hour, and other things that the minds of the unimaginative conceive of innovations, the inventor drew from his wallet $3,000 that the city of Philadelphia had just paid him for his steamboat, and said the carping critic could transfer the "roll" to his own pocket, if he could produce a horse that would run faster for five miles than a steam wagon that Evans would build. The size of the roll was too much for the pessimist, and he betook himself and his criticisms off.

So we see that as there was a first automobile, so was there a first automobile enthusiast on automobile speed. Why it is that motordom hasn't erected a monument to Oliver Evans for his abiding faith in the future of the motor car as a speed demon, is up to motordom to explain.

Automobile Apathy Century Old.

Oliver Evans tried but was unable to get any one interested in developing his wagon run by an engine into an improved horseless carriage. The minds of that day regarded the practicability of his invention with as much skepticism as we would regard an invention to visit Mars, if exhibited in our day.

So Evans gave up any idea of improving his self-running wagon, became busy with an iron foundry which people could understand, and died rich.

There was a measure of justification for the lack of popular imagination and vision toward the automobile in both England and America when the first samples appeared. They were slow, noisy, erratic in performance, and positively dangerous—threatening explosions, collisions, and all sorts of dire things—and it was natural that people should predict their failure.

So progress in the development of the horseless carriage lagged. It was twenty years after Evans' Philadelphia exhibition when it was next heard from. Then the scene of operations shifted again to England.

In 1824, W. H. James, who had patented a water tube boiler for locomotives, built a passenger coach, of which each drive wheel was revolved by two cylinders receiving steam by means of a pipe from a boiler.

A pressure of 200 pounds of steam to the inch was maintained. The equivalent of differential action was supplied by independent application of power to the two drive wheels. The coach accommodated twenty persons. The contrivance ran satisfactorily on trials, and James secured financial backing and built another coach weighing 6,000 pounds which ran 12 to 15 miles an hour.

But the higher the rate of speed, the worse off the early automobile builder was. Although James equipped his coach with laminated steel springs, the road shocks and vibration stopped it every few miles. Steam joints and connections were broken as fast as they could be put together. The great need was a method of shock absorption, and either no one knew that this was the key to the problem, or, if it was realized, no one knew the remedy. So James failed to make the auto-coach a success, and died in the poorhouse.

A year after James built his first motor-coach in England—in 1825—Thomas Blanchard of Springfield, Mass., revived the horseless carriage subject which, in America, had been last experimented with by Oliver Evans in 1804.

Blanchard built a road vehicle that was one of the best produced up to that time. It was easy of manipulation and climbed hills successfully. Blanchard took out a patent on it, but when he started to find people who would buy a completed carriage he could discover none. Nobody wanted it. And so Blanchard's efforts ceased.

At the time James was building his two coaches, and after Blanchard had given up trying to interest Americans in his invention, a Frenchman named Pecqueur was experimenting on phases of the auto-carriage. He discovered the principle of the "differential," the balance mechanism which enables one wheel to revolve faster than the other in turning corners. He invented a planet gearing in this connection, which was the origin of the idea of the differential, and applied it to a steam wagon which he built in 1828. The differential of today is based on the principle discovered by Pecqueur.

While Pecqueur was evolving this invention, Goldsworthy Gurney in England made a car which was a practical failure in about everything except that it demonstrated that sufficient friction between the drive wheels and the road-bed could be created to produce propulsion. A trip of almost 200 miles from London and return was made in 1828 by Gurney in the second vehicle he built, in which the engine was concealed in the rear. His car made 12 miles an hour for part of the trip.

From this time—1828 to 1840—the automobile really had a vogue in England. A number of them were made and run as passenger carriers. For four months a motor carriage made the nine mile trip from Gloucester to Cheltenham four times a day. The "Infant" built by Walter Hancock made trips between London and Stratford. The "Era," also made by Hancock, ran from London to Greenwich. To such an extent did the auto-bus business develop, that speed of 30 miles an hour was claimed, and one conveyance in 1834 ran over 1,700 miles without repairs or readjustment. At least, that was the claim made, and as a claim it has a familiar sound. The twentieth century automobile manufacturers who claim a run of so many thousand miles without repairs to this and that, have here a precedent for it that is as old as the industry.

But there was one feature about these early English motor busses that was their undoing. They weighed three tons and over, and the wheel rims were metal. The diameter of the wheels was six feet. The rubber tire was unthought of. The effect on roads of running a 3-ton, metal rimmed vehicle, carrying eleven to twenty passengers, was disastrous, and Parliament, incited by horse owners and others, legislated them out of existence by making the toll charges prohibitive. Where the toll was $1 for horse drawn vehicles it was made $10 for steam auto buses. The consequence was that their manufacture and operation ceased about 1840.

In 1878 Bollee built a steam omnibus which ran between Paris and Vienna, making 22 miles an hour. In this car was reached the highest efficiency the art had attained up to that time. Practically an identical car was built in 188065 by Bollee, which was entered by him 15 years later and won honors in the Paris-Bordeaux race.

In 1879 the automobile development germ returned to America.

In this brief sketch showing the struggle of auto-mechanism to advance, from the very first inspiration of Cugnot about 1770, we must be impressed by the determination with which the

IDEA OF AUTO-MECHANICAL PERFECTION PERSISTED. THIS PERSISTENCE WAS SO DETERMINED IN THE FACE OF ALL OBSTACLES AND OPPOSITION THAT IT IS ALMOST EERIE.

IT WAS JUST AS IF SOME FORCE OF NATURE WAS STRUGGLING TO BREAK THROUGH THE CRUST OF MAN'S CONSCIOUSNESS. OR SHALL WE CREDIT IT TO MAN, AND SAY, RATHER, THAT IT WAS MAN'S MIND THAT WAS THE IMPELLING FORCE IN THE PERSISTENT ATTEMPTS TO READ A MECHANICAL RIDDLE?

WHATEVER THE IMPELLING FORCE, WHETHER MAN OR NATURE, MAN HEEDED ITS BEHESTS AND CONTINUED HIS EFFORTS.

IN 1879 AN AMERICAN DID A THING WHICH HAS HAD MUCH TO DO WITH GIVING THE UNITED STATES ITS LONG DELAYED START IN THE AUTOMOBILE INDUSTRY. THIS MAN WAS GEORGE B. SELDEN OF ROCHESTER, N. Y. HE APPLIED FOR THE FIRST PATENT FOR THE GASOLINE MOTOR, AS THE DRIVING FORCE OF A ROAD VEHICLE. THIS WAS BEFORE ANY AUTOMOBILE HAD BEEN EQUIPPED WITH AN INTERNAL COMBUSTION HYDRO-CARBON MOTOR. THIS MOTOR HAD, HOWEVER, BEEN IN USE FOR SOME TIME IN RUNNING STATIONARY ENGINES.

THE BICYCLE HAD, AT THAT TIME, BEEN AN ACKNOWLEDGED SUCCESS, AND IN CONSIDERABLE USE FOR SEVEN OR EIGHT YEARS, AND HAD HAD A GREAT DEAL OF INFLUENCE IN IMPROVING ROADS. BETTER ROADS CAUSED PEOPLE TO LOOK MORE FAVORABLY ON THE POSSIBILITIES OF THE MOTOR VEHICLE.

SELDEN BUILT A GASOLINE MOTOR UNDER THE SPECIFICATIONS CONTAINED IN HIS APPLICATION FOR A PATENT, AND IT PERFORMED SATISFACTORILY IN EXPERIMENTS. BUT HE DID NOT BUILD AN AUTOMOBILE CONTAINING THE GASOLINE MOTOR. HE DID NOT SECURE HIS PATENT UNTIL 1895, 16 YEARS AFTER HE HAD MADE APPLICATION FOR IT.

IN THOSE SIXTEEN YEARS HE WAS ENDEAVORING TO INTEREST CAPITAL, WHILE AT THE SAME TIME HE WAS PERFECTING HIS MOTOR. WHILE THE USE OF BICYCLES HAD IMPROVED ROADS AND THIS IMPROVEMENT CAUSED A MORE FAVORABLE POPULAR VIEW OF THE POSSIBILITY THAT AUTOMOBILES MIGHT BE MADE SUCCESSFULLY, A NEW MOTIVE POWER APPEARED ON THE HORIZON JUST AT THIS TIME.

IT WAS ELECTRICITY. IT WAS IN 1890, ELEVEN YEARS AFTER SELDEN HAD APPLIED FOR A PATENT FOR A GASOLINE MOTOR, AND WHILE HE WAS STILL WRESTLING WITH THE PROBLEM OF GETTING CAPITAL TO AID HIM, that reports that the storage battery had been more nearly perfected became rife.

Men to whom Selden went for financial aid feared that even if the gasoline motor was feasible, it might be overshadowed by the storage battery, and held off. Selden even went abroad to raise money, but had no more success there than here.

Although an inventor and a skilled mechanic, Selden lacked salesmanship ability. He was handicapped by impatience and irascibility, and his predictions of the success of his gasoline motor, its general adoption, and the extent to which automobiles would in the future be used, were regarded by people with whom he talked as so extravagant that they bluntly declared he was crazy, and avoided him.

He had proceeded so far on one occasion in interesting a Rochester business man, that he had him in his store and was on the point of getting him to put up $5,000, when he made a simple remark that completely "spilled the beans."

He said: "Jim, you and I will live to see more carriages on Main Street run by motor than are now drawn by horses."

The prospective investor looked at Selden for half a minute, and came to a conclusion expressed in these words:

"George, you are crazy, and I won't have anything to do with your scheme," and with this ultimatum the man stalked out of the store.

Twenty-five years later this man met Selden, and, extending his hand, said: "Well, George, you were right years ago when you said there would be more automobiles in Main Street than horses."

But Selden ignored the man's extended hand, and with passion thrilling in his tones said: "Yes, and I wasn't so —— crazy as you and the other fools said I was," and walked off. And he never spoke to the man afterward.

Selden's patent could have been issued any time within the sixteen years that he let it lie dormant. He kept the application alive at the patent office by legitimate methods, and his reason for not bringing the matter to a head was that

At no time in those sixteen years was he ready to manufacture under it, and he put off the actual issuance until such time as he was prepared to take full advantage of the privileges it conferred.

He was alive to the fact that the years of a patent are numbered, and he aimed to time the issue so that the patent would not expire before he could derive the benefits from it.

It was in 1895 that the patent was issued, and in 1900 Selden disposed of it to the Electric Vehicle Company of New Jersey.

In the meantime, the development of electric motor vehicles had begun, and in 1885, Benz, a German, built the first road vehicle to be run by the internal-combustion, hydro-carbon motor. It was a tricycle, and its motor was single-cylindered, four-cycled, after the type of an engine developed in 1876, in Germany, by Otto, and water cooled. It had electric ignition and a mechanical carburetor. Benz secured a patent in 1886 on his invention and it ran successfully, making ten miles an hour. Benz was limited to the use of certain streets in Mannheim, Germany, for running his machine, out of deference to the tendency to nerves of horses and their drivers or riders. This tricycle by Benz was the forerunner of the Benz automobile. This is one of the most successful and popular cars in Germany—and before the war, in all Europe. The first automobile imported into the United States was a Benz car brought to the Chicago World's Fair in 1893. Up to 1917 the Benz car was an entrant in most automobile speed contests.

While Benz was perfecting the gasoline motor in its attachment to the tricycle, Gottlieb Daimler, another German, was producing, in 1885, the motor-cycle. Daimler had devoted himself sedulously to the problem of reducing the weight and increasing the power of the gas engine, in order to adapt it to high efficiency road vehicles. He invented the hot tube ignition to take the place of ignition by flame. By regulation of the heat of the tube, the compressed charge of hydro-carbon vapor could be fired automatically at a specific point in the cycle. Through the increased speed thus produced the size and weight of the motor could be reduced.

The Daimler motor was a big step in advance, as was proved by the supremacy which the German and French automobile makers at once attained. The French secured rights to the

Daimler motor and operated under them with such success that from 1889 to 1894, before the United States had really waked up to motor car making, they were beginning to put out gasoline automobiles successfully.

America Builds Steam and Electric Cars.

At this time, we, in this country, were following the steam and storage battery fetishes. The first steam car in the United States that might be called modern was built by S. H. Roper of Massachusetts, in 1889. In 1900, steam car building in America gave promise of disputing the gasoline car records then being made in France, but by 1905 the gasoline car manufacturers had taken the cue from the European gasoline successes, and this form of motor came to the front.

Contemporaneously with the activities in steam car building in the United States, was the pioneer electric car construction era.

The first electric automobile was built in 1891, and made its first exhibition appearance in the streets of Chicago in September, 1892. The builder of this, the first electric driven vehicle, was William Morrison of Des Moines, Iowa. It was bought by J. B. McDonald, president of the American Battery Company, Chicago. Description of the street scenes attending the showing of this car bring home to us the extent to which an automobile was a novelty so short a time ago, comparatively, as 1892. "Ever since its arrival," said the *Western Electrician* of September 17, 1892, "it has attracted the greatest attention. The sight of a well loaded carriage moving along the streets at a spanking pace, with no horses in front, and apparently with nothing on board to give it motion, was one that has been too much, even for the wide-awake Chicagoan. In passing through the business section, way had to be cleared by the police for the passage of the carriage."

To think that this description fits a scene enacted during the period of the present generation! Eighty-eight years before in Philadelphia, Oliver Evans' steam propelled wagon, bearing in triumph a flatboat surmounted by an engine, moved along Market Street with no horses in front, and was a sight that was too much for the Philadelphian.

The world "do move," but very slowly, and this 88-year span of time is practically the measure of the period consumed by automobile development to the point where a motor carriage would really run, and keep on running.

The date of the building of the first American gasoline automobile that ran was 1892. The man who performed the feat was Charles E. Duryea. He had the assistance of his brother, Frank Duryea, but what was more, he had the benefit of knowledge of what had been accomplished in Europe in the gasoline motor field.

Panhard, Levassor, Peugeot, De Dion, Bouton, and Serpollet were Frenchmen who had done things with gasoline cars, all (except Serpollet and Levassor) principally through the manufacture of finished cars. Levassor conceived the idea of a central frame to carry the power plant, and thus solved the problem of road shock.

Serpollet had done more. He had invented the flash boiler, reviving an art the English had previously discovered, which made the use of dry or superheated steam possible. Higher pressure could be used, water economies effected and weight reduced.

When Duryea and others, about 1892, gave concentrated thought to gasoline propulsion, all the problems of automobile making had found solution, except two. They were a method of cushioning wheel rims, and some method by which the motor could be so placed that it would be immune from shocks and vibrations.

So, when Duryea, in 1892, built the first American gasoline car that would run successfully, he merely "assembled" the ideas that had then accumulated.

The first auto-race in the world was run from Paris to Rouen, about 80 miles. It was run in July, 1894. There were 46 cars entered, of which twelve only were steam cars. The Petit-Journal, a Parisian newspaper, was the organizer and patron of the race. The winners were all equipped with the Daimler gasoline motor.

A little over one year later—Thanksgiving Day, 1895—the first American automobile race was run from Chicago to Waukegan. The organizer and patron was a newspaper—the

Chicago Times-Herald. Of two entrants, the "Buggyaut" of Charles E. Duryea was one.

Duryea built his first car in 1892.

Henry Ford built his in 1893.

Elwood Haynes built his in 1894.

There were but four gasoline cars in the United States in 1896—Duryea, Ford, Haynes, and Benz, the last being the German car which was imported.

With the accomplishments of the builders of steam, electric and gasoline motored vehicles at this time—1895—the practical success of horseless carriages had been definitely settled. Practically all fundamental problems had been solved. To make them finally an accepted addition to the world's methods of transportation in general use, two things only were needed.

One was the development of perfecting devices, such as rubber tires, the production of which began about 1889; and the other was the general acceptance of automobiles by the people—a cordial, popular approval, manifested by their purchase and use. And while the development to greater perfection could be left to work itself out, the popular approval to the point of enthusiastic general adoption was another matter.

Inventors could develop, even if it took over a hundred years, a complete, perfect machine, finally. But human doubts, mental apathy, and man's opposition can be overcome by only one means—enthusiasm.

Enthusiasm is to man's opposing mind what the oxyhydrogen flame is to steel, and it is one of the potent forces that will burn itself into mentality.

Around the period of 1893-1898, the attitude of the mass of the people in this country toward the automobile was one of good natured toleration, but indifference. A few of the "class" were interested and convinced that the automobile had arrived, but the "mass" believed it was a passing fad, and from its practical side, of particular interest chiefly to mechanics. If, in its opinion, the automobile had any future, it was as a luxury of the rich.

The people could not sense what they feel now—the value of the automobile in time, health and recreation, and in its possibilities as a factor in economics. They saw the disadvantages of owning an automobile, but were without appreciation of its benefits.

So one of the most interesting facts in the history of the development of the motor car is that the first American made gasoline automobile sold in the United States was disposed of March 24, 1898. The sale of steamers and electrics had been going on for several years before, but not very extensively.

This fact of the date of the first sale of a gasoline motor car fixes clearly that the use of automobiles in the United States practically increased from one car to over three million, in less than twenty years.

The first American gasoline car thus sold was disposed of by Alexander Winton to Robert Allison of Port Carbon, Pa.

So that, while Duryea completed his car in 1892, Ford his in 1893, and Haynes his in 1894, it was six, five and four years, respectively, later, that the first gasoline car was purchased in the United States.

From 1898, the time of the sale of the Winton car, dates substantially the development of the automobile industry in this country.

Beginning with this date, the first real enthusiasm was put into the sale of cars.

Enthusiasm had not existed before. Confidence, which is the mother of enthusiasm, had hesitated and halted. But now confidence believed the automobile was a reality—all doubts had been resolved—and confidence bade enthusiasm run, not creep, crawl or walk; and we see how enthusiasm obeyed. In the enthusiasm displayed in the manufacture and sale of automobiles today, we are disposed to think it does more than run, that it actually flies.

CHAPTER III.

COMMERCIALIZING THE MOTOR VEHICLE.

IN THE PRODUCTION OF THE AUTOMOBILE, AMERICA DID COMPARATIVELY LITTLE IN THE FUNDAMENTALS OF INVENTION WHICH ARE NOW FOUND IN THE MODERN PERFECTED CAR.

SELDEN INVENTED THE THREE-CYLINDER GASOLINE ENGINE, BY WHICH THE RAPID REVOLUTION OF THE CRANKSHAFT OF HIS DAY WAS CONVERTED INTO SLOWER BUT HIGHER POWERED MOTION OF DRIVE WHEELS.

WHITE INVENTED A GENERATOR FOR STEAM CARS.

HAYNES WAS RESPONSIBLE FOR A DISCOVERY THAT CAUSED ALLOY AND SPECIALLY HEAT-TREATED STEEL TO BE INTRODUCED, AND KNIGHT PRODUCED A SUPERIOR MOTOR.

BUT THESE WERE DISCOVERIES, INVENTIONS OR IMPROVEMENTS THAT WERE SUPPLEMENTAL AND PERFECTING, NOT ELEMENTAL.

IT WAS CHIEFLY THE ENGLISH, THE FRENCH AND THE GERMANS, WITH THE EXCEPTION OF EVANS OF PHILADELPHIA, WHO FIRST CONCEIVED THE IDEA OF THE HORSELESS CARRIAGE, AND HELPED IT TO ITS FINAL DEVELOPMENT BY A SERIES OF SUCCESSIVE INVENTIONS. THE NAMES OF CUGNOT, TREVITHICK, JAMES, PECQUEUR, HANCOCK, GURNEY, LENOIR, BOLLEE, BENZ, DAIMLER, LEVASSOR AND SERPOLLET SHOULD FORM THE NOMENCLATIVE SETTING OF COMMEMORATIVE FRIEZES ON THE WALLS OF THE GRATEFUL MOTOR CLUBS OF THE FUTURE, AS THOSE OF LISZT, BEETHOVEN, WAGNER, GOUNOD, HANDEL, MASSENET, BACH, MENDELSSOHN, GRIEG AND CHOPIN TAKE HONORED PLACE IN THE SHRINES OF MUSIC, THE "HEAVENLY MAID."

EVEN IN THE PRODUCTION OF AUTOMOBILES IN ANY QUANTITY FOR USE—THE COMMERCIALIZING OF THE IDEA THEY REPRESENT—THE UNITED STATES DID NOT LEAD AT FIRST. THIS HONOR BELONGS TO FRANCE, AS DOES THE ORIGINAL CONCEPTION BY CUGNOT OF THE HORSELESS VEHICLE.

THE FIRST STEAM CARS MANUFACTURED IN THE UNITED STATES, ON ANY BASIS ENTITLING THEIR MANUFACTURE TO THE DIGNITY OF A BUSINESS, WERE MADE AFTER 1894, AND THE NAMES OF RIKER, WHITE AND STANLEY ARE THE PROMINENT ONES IN THE STEAM AUTOMOBILE field. Electric carriages were sold as commercial commodities in comparatively small quantities, beginning with 1897, and the first American gasoline car sold in the United States was made and sold by Alexander Winton in 1898.

Beginning prior to 1892, the French were selling automobiles by the hundred, while manufacturers in America were selling them by the dozen. Panhard and Peugeot were selling gasoline cars, and DeDion-Bouton was putting the steam automobile on the world's market.

But the race is not always to the swiftest. While France started bravely on its commercialization of the automobile, and had in its favor what were then good roads of an old and well settled country to run them over, and perhaps the thriftiest people of any nation to buy them, there were causes existing in the United States destined to make of it the greatest automobile producing country in the world, and its people the largest users of the new invention, while at the same time operating to cause the United States to sell more cars outside its confines, to Europe and elsewhere, than are sold by any other country.

And inasmuch as these underlying causes, while explaining the supremacy of this country to this date in the manufacture and sale of automobiles, also explain the reason for believing that the future of the automobile business will dwarf the proportions it has up to this time reached, they will bear analysis.

In the first place, European manufacturers of automobiles, as well as of other products generally, with the possible exception in a degree, of the Germans, are bound hand and foot, and therefore handicapped, by tradition and convention. They make the automobile, especially the French and English, so solidly, with such fidelity to tradition and with such conscientious care as to detail, elaboration and finish, that the price to the buyer, when it is put beside that of a similar American made product, will not meet competition.

The American has a knack of turning out an article which is mechanically correct, has the wearing qualities, but is simpler in detail, and hence can be sold at a lower cost. Simplicity is the American manufacturer's keynote.

Back of this is business organization system, standardization of parts used in the automobile, and that high order of constructive and executive talent that gives the American business man the distinctive reputation he enjoys and enables him successfully to compete in price and quality with the rest of the world. There has been a rare combination of inventive and business abilities in American automobile manufacturers.

American mechanical genius has been given great credit, but wherein is it any greater than that of the German, French or English? In one particular—its simplicity. The Europeans are elaborate—the Americans plain and simple.

It is possible that no European manufacturer would have conceived an automobile embodying the essentials of small size, simplicity and speed represented by a Ford car. His tradition and training would have impelled him to elaboration in size and finish. In this, he is, of course, moulded by European needs and tastes which differ, in many respects, from those of the people of this country.

He does not possess the American's practical vision in successful salesmanship. Ford made his car with an eye to quantity. He was not only an inventor, but a salesman. As he worked on his motor, he worked on the problems of sales—producing a car that would sell to the largest number. The larger the number sold, the smaller the price could be made.

"Large sales and small profits" has been a principle which has made many American fortunes. Note how this same idea of Ford has been followed by Willys in the Overland, Olds in the Reo, the makers of the Maxwell, and half a score of other manufacturers in varying degrees, causing the gamut of prices of the most popular cars to run from $360 to $1,200 each.

This is one reason why the American car could invade England and her dominions beyond the seas, why Ford has factories in the British Isles and Canada, and why our yearly exports of automobiles have increased in the last five years over $100,000,000 in value.

Other reasons that make us an exporting country of automobiles through their low prices are our natural resources of iron, steel, lumber, coal and alloys, enabling us, by their plentifulness and accessibility, to manufacture at cheap cost, thus offsetting the higher price we pay for labor in this country than the European manufacturers pay.

But the biggest factor in the lead which the United States has taken in the production of automobiles, both for export and consumption within her own borders, is the universal method of standardizing in manufacture, adopted by the automobile producers of the nation.

The manufacturers of this country shine in the field of cost production, in the economies of purchase of raw materials, in the method of manufacture, and in marketing their product.

Advertising's Help in Making the Automobile.

The extent to which economic methods of purchase of raw materials—getting the price down—economic standardization of manufacture, inventing short cuts as it were—affects production cost, is shown in the fact that the automobile industry ranks almost at the top in the manufactures of the United States in the per cent of value added by manufacture to the cost of material.

The per cent of value added by manufacture to cost of material in automobile production is 71 per cent, against 66 per cent in cotton goods, 55 per cent in iron and steel products, 51 per cent in boots and shoes, 16 per cent in flour and grist mill products, and 12 per cent in slaughtering and meat packing.

Strange as it may sound when first stated, advertising is primarily the base of this result. We know that the first principle of lowered cost is buying in quantities; that if we buy for 100, the cost for each is lower than the cost for one; if for 1,000 it is lower than the cost for each of 100, and so on.

So, when Ford buys the materials for 533,921 cars, which was the number he sold in 1916, he gets the price of the cost of each of these more than a half million cars down to a less price than if he bought material for 1,708 cars, the number he made in 1904, or even 168,220, the number he made in 1913.

This is patent to any one who ever heard of wholesale and retail prices.

But how did Ford find a sale for 533,921 cars in 1916?

By advertising.

The first thing a manufacturer must do to lower the cost of production of the single unit is to make in quantities.

How to insure the disposal of that quantity has been the big problem that American automobile manufacturers have had to solve. The solution was at hand. It was advertising. The commercializing of automobiles with the speed and to the extent to which it was done between 1900 and 1917 could not have been successfully accomplished before this period, because the recognition of the value of advertising had not become widespread up to that time.

Advertising had gone through a process of development that was as slow as that of the automobile business. Both arts emerged from darkness into light at about the same time. Here is evidence that a very bright and smart set of men engaged in automobile production at the very outset.

They were mechanical, they were versed in business methods, and they were conscious of the value of advertising.

This combination of knowledge by the men engaged in it has made the automobile industry a record breaker in point of the time consumed in its development. It has made it stand out as unparalleled by any other industry in this country in the speed with which it progressed from final experimentation to an established recognized enterprise, involving mammoth investment of capital and huge profits.

That the automobile business has been the most extensively advertised business of any in which we are engaged, almost anyone will concede from knowledge gained from his own observation.

Advertising is like the rainbow—many hued. It may be one form, or it may be another. It may whisper, or it may shout. We must concede that the advertising the automobile promoters have done was more largely of the shouting than the whispering kind. That is not to their discredit—rather otherwise. The distinct injunction to advertise is contained in the Bible. It was: "To so let your good work shine that," etc., and the people of scriptural days were admonished not to hide their light under a bushel.

Newspapers are said, somewhat carelessly, to have made the automobile business. It is not exactly fair to make this statement so sweepingly. They did for it a good deal more than they did for any other line of industry, and are still doing it.

They never devoted the space that they gave to the automobile to railroads, steamboats, the telephone, street railways, oil, lumber, mining, meat packing, or any other commercial industry. It was not, necessarily, that the automobile manufacturers, in all cases, asked for this liberal treatment by the newspapers.

It was that newspapers volunteered it. One started it, and others followed. The spell which the idea contained in the automobile weaves over men and women was cast equally over the editors and publishers in the United States. In recognition of the novelty of the automobile, they laid liberal offerings of free space on the altar of motordom. Its peculiar exhilaration penetrated the editorial sanctum, and in this distinctive exhilaration the automobile has had no parallel except in golf.

It has been quite generally accepted as an axiom that if you give, you receive. We see this statement proved in a hundred ways. A pleasant smile begets a smile. A good deed is matched in kind. No better reason for this exists, probably, than that it is ingrained in us to hate to be under obligations to anybody. So when we get a smile we promptly pay it back and are square, just as we invite to lunch a man who invited us to lunch. We are very particular about this.

The automobile manufacturers were not lacking in this trait, common to human nature. When publishers put their stamp of approval on the motor car and unreservedly threw open their columns to the progress made in its improvements and production, manufacturers appreciated and reciprocated.

The result has been that more money has been spent in advertising in the automobile business in the United States than has been spent in any other single line of enterprise. Possibly the nearest approach to it has been patent medicine, or the promotion of various enterprises.

And it has paid—every automobile maker, and every salesman will admit this as a matter of course. They will admit it because they know it to be so—a knowledge derived in their own experience.

The psychology of advertising shows that there are two principal things involved in making advertising profitably productive. One is that it informs, the other that it persuades. If the mind is informed of what an automobile is, what it does, and all the advantages and benefits it confers, it has a basis to work on, and from this working basis it will evolve conclusions.

The state of the mind in the conclusive stage is fallow field for persuasive effort.

In the advertising given in this country to the automobile which has placed millions of motor cars in the ownership of people in the United States, not counting those exported, the publishers of our journals have supplied the information, and the manufacturer the persuasion.

It is this double teamwork which, supplementing the business ability of our manufacturers, has put us in the front rank as automobile producers. But baldly to say that the newspapers made the automobile is not giving full credit to the other causes which contribute to our success in this line of enterprise. It has been a combination of causes working together which has made the automobile.

United States a Fertile Field.

There have been other forms of advertising used in automobile selling, besides space in publications, and they are forms the value of which cannot be discounted. "A satisfied customer is the best advertisement" is one of the oldest slogans of advertising. And it is true. The automobile manufacturers of the United States know it is true, and have been guided by it.

Road races, speed and endurance contests, employment of racing drivers with records, automobile shows, outdoor displays—all have been forms of advertising employed in the industry, and all have played their part and exerted their influence to one common end—that of putting the industry in the United States on the highest pinnacle it has attained anywhere in the world in seventeen years.

And while full credit must be given the vision and capabilities of the manufacturers, and the productive value of advertising in all forms, meed for the results can not be withheld from that element, which, in the final analysis,

MAKES ALL THINGS POSSIBLE—THE PEOPLE, THE BASE AND GROUNDWORK ON WHICH ALL SUCCESSFUL INDUSTRIAL STRUCTURES ARE ERECTED.

ALL THE BUSINESS ABILITY OF ALL THE AUTOMOBILE MAKERS, HOWEVER GREAT, AND ALL THE ADVERTISING, HOWEVER CONVINCING, THAT COULD BE WRITTEN, COULD NOT HAVE MADE THE AUTOMOBILE BUSINESS OF TODAY IF THE PEOPLE HAD NOT TAKEN HOLD OF THE AUTOMOBILE AND PUT THEIR STAMP OF APPROVAL ON IT.

"POWER OF THE PRESS"—WHAT IS IT BUT THE "POWER OF THE PEOPLE" EXPRESSED ON PAPER? POWER OF THE PEOPLE—THE FORCE THAT REVOLVES THE WORLD, REVOLVED THE WHEELS OF MILLIONS OF AUTOMOBILES, AND WILL GO ON TURNING THE WHEELS OF MILLIONS MORE.

THE PEOPLE OF THE UNITED STATES SUPPLIED THE FERTILE FIELD IN WHICH THE AMERICAN AUTOMOBILE GREW AND BLOSSOMED.

THE REASON FRANCE, ALTHOUGH IT TOOK THE LEAD IN THE COMMERCIALIZATION OF THE MOTOR CAR, COULD NOT HOLD IT IN THE RACE WITH THIS COUNTRY IS TO BE FOUND IN THE DIFFERENCE BETWEEN THE PEOPLES OF THE TWO COUNTRIES.

FRANCE HAD GOOD ROADS—HAS HAD THEM AS HAS EUROPE FOR HUNDREDS OF YEARS. THE FRENCH HAD MONEY—THEY ARE THE GREATEST SAVERS IN THE WORLD.

BUT IF YOU PUT YOUR MONEY IN RENTES OR SAVINGS BANKS, YOU DO NOT SPEND IT FOR AUTOMOBILES OR ANYTHING ELSE. THE REASON THE FRENCH HAVE MONEY IS THE REASON THEY DO NOT BUY AUTOMOBILES.

NO PEOPLE IN THE WORLD HAVE LEARNED, AS HAVE AMERICANS, TO SPEND MONEY TO MAKE MONEY. NO PEOPLE IN THE WORLD TAKE THE CHANCES AMERICANS DO, AND NO PEOPLE WIN AS THE AMERICANS DO. IN THIS IS FOUND ONE OF MANY CAUSES FOR THE COMMERCIAL SUCCESS OF THE AUTOMOBILE IN AMERICA.

THE AMERICAN IS GOOD TO HIMSELF AS IS THE MAN OF NO OTHER NATIONALITY. HE IS FURTHER ADVANCED IN GENERAL KNOWLEDGE, MOSTLY GAINED BY EXPERIENCE THROUGH INTERCOMMUNICATION WITH HIS FELLOWS. HIS BON CAMARADERIE IS EFFERVESCENT, GIVING HIM OPPORTUNITIES TO LEARN THINGS DENIED TO THE SELF-RESTRAINED EUROPEAN. HIS SCHOOL IS THE BROAD SCHOOL OF THE WORLD. HE DOESN'T HAVE TO TRAVEL TO SEE THE WORLD; THE WORLD IS IN AMERICA AND COMES TO HIM.

So, with the opportunities natural to a new country, with the standards of living and the mode of thought that they are in the United States, the 103,000,000 people of continental United States are a market for automobiles that dwarf the 464,000,000 people of Europe.

What such a market has been during the last decade and a half may be gathered from the fact that in the last sixteen years the population of the United States increased at a greater rate than ever in its history. The increase of the people of the United States in the sixteen years the automobile industry has been commercialized, was 25,887,904. In the previous twenty years the increase was 25,838,792.

People without money can not buy automobiles, so what has been the increase in wealth in the United States in this same period?

In the last twelve years it has been $99,221,764,315.

Staggering, you say? Rather, when you know that the increase in wealth in the United States in the last twelve years was nearly double the increase in the twenty years which preceded the last twelve years.

No epoch in the world's history, therefore, was so favorable as the period of 1900-1917 for commercializing the automobile. It was timed just to the moment for quick and dramatic success. The period was coincident with the high water marks reached in the increase of population and in the nation's money-making. Advertising had reached a stage of development it had not attained before.

Stars in Their Courses Fought for the Automobile.

We must credit enthusiasm for some of the influence in the success of the industry. We will have to admit that it is present in the factory and in the selling mart, in the shows and on the road. A satisfied customer, the best advertisement, finds expression in the loyal recommendation an owner gives his own make of car; enthusiasm of maker, of salesman, of owner—it runs along the line, and if advertising is the gasoline which makes the car go, enthusiasm is the oil which keeps the bearings of the industry lubricated.

The year 1898 saw the first real attempts of manufacturers in the United States, either of gasoline, electric or steam cars, to make them in any quantity.

The gasoline cars that were pioneers were the Duryea, the Ford and the Haynes, but until 1898 these were distinctly still in the field of experimentation. Ford personally built a car run by a gasoline motor of the two-cylinder, four-cycle type of his own construction, and this car ran 25 miles an hour. Ford was second only to Duryea who constructed the first gasoline car built in the United States.

Duryea persisted in producing a buggy type of car, and failed to get any sale for it. Ford and Haynes had no better luck in finding purchasers for their cars.

Alexander Winton entered the field after Duryea, Ford and Haynes, and in 1898 sold the first gasoline car that was bought for use in the United States.

Ford built his first car in 1893. It was not a perfect car, but better than any which had preceded it. He built his second car in 1895, with a 4 × 4 two-cylinder, four-cycle motor. In this year he organized the Detroit Automobile Company with a capital of $50,000. Ford owned one-sixth interest, and drew $100 a month salary as chief engineer.

In the six years Ford remained with the Detroit Automobile Company it put out only two or three cars. In 1901 Ford severed his connection with the company, which shortly became the Cadillac Automobile Company, and is now the Cadillac Motor Car Company. The Cadillac has had a successful career, and is one of the cars of which a particularly large number has been sold.

Leaving the Detroit Automobile Company, Ford started a machine shop of his own, and in 1902 produced a car with a 90-inch wheel base, and which is now regarded as standard gauge, using the two cylinders, 4 × 4, and a double opposed engine.

After much difficulty he got money from half a dozen persons and organized the Ford Motor Company with a capital of $100,000. At first he owned only 25½ per cent of the stock, but later he borrowed $175,000 and bought 25½ per cent more, and still later by paying 700 per cent of its face value, secured 7½

PER CENT MORE, WHICH MAKES HIS HOLDING IN THE COMPANY AT THIS TIME 58½ PER CENT OF THE STOCK.

THE FIRST FORD CAR TO BE A COMMERCIAL SUCCESS WAS PUT OUT IN 1903, AND THE RECORD OF PRODUCTION OF FORD CARS TO DATE IS AS FOLLOWS:

Year. No. Cars.

Year	No. Cars
1904	1,708
1905	1,695
1906	1,599
1907	8,423
1908	6,398
1909	10,607
1910	18,664
1911	34,528
1912	78,440
1913	168,220
1914	248,307
1915	308,213
1916	533,921

IN 1916 THE FORD PRODUCTION WAS OVER ONE-SIXTH OF THE 3,000,000 CARS IN USE IN THE UNITED STATES. IN THAT YEAR HE PRODUCED NEARLY ONE-THIRD OF ALL THE PASSENGER CARS MADE IN THAT YEAR.

FORD'S CAR WAS A SMALL, LOW PRICED CAR FROM THE START. HAYNES' WAS A LARGER AND HIGHER PRICED CAR. WINTON'S WAS LIKEWISE A LARGE AND MORE EXPENSIVE CAR.

A RAIN OF AUTOMOBILE MAKERS.

THE YEAR OF THE SPANISH-AMERICAN WAR—1898—SAW THE BEGINNING OF A VERITABLE RAIN OF AUTOMOBILE MANUFACTURERS IN THE UNITED STATES. IN THAT YEAR THE STANLEY, STEARNS, THOMAS, MATHESON, WINTON, AND THE WAVERLEY COMPANY ENTERED THE FIELD.

In 1899, there appeared the Locomobile Company, Olds, Baker-Electric and Pierce-Racine (later absorbed by J. I. Case and now the Case car).

In 1900, Packard, Peerless, Glide, National Electric, Lambert, Elmore, Babcock, Jackson, Knox and Lane were entrants in the lists.

In 1901, Acme, Gaeth, Pierce-Arrow, White, Royal Tourist, Stevens-Duryea, Waltham-Orient, Pope-Toledo, Welch, Pullman and Rambler.

In 1902, Cadillac, Franklin, Pope, Studebaker, Sultan, Okey, Walter and Schacht.

In 1903, Ford, Auburn, Overland, Moline, Premier, Corbin, Bergdall, Holsman, Columbus and Chadwick.

In 1904, Buick, Cleveland, American Napier, Stoddard-Dayton, Marmon, Mitchell, Jewel, McIntyre, Pittsburgh Electric, Ranch & Lang and Simplex.

In 1905, Alco, American, Dorris, Johnson, Jonz, Kisselcar, Maxwell, Monarch, Reo, Studebaker, Garford and American Mors.

In 1906, Anderson, A. B. C., Cartercar, Brunn, Thomas-Detroit, Kearns, Sterling, Mora, Moon, Pennsylvania, Palmer & Singer and Staver.

In 1907, Albany, Atlas, Brush, Bertolet, Byrider, Carter, Chalmers, Coppock, De Luxe, Oakland, Regal, Selden, Speedwell, Interstate, Lozier and Great Western.

In 1908, Sharp-Arrow, Pittsburgh 6, Crown Midland, Rider-Lewis, Paige-Detroit, Velie, Cole, E. M. F. and Hupmobile.

In 1909, Hudson, Advance, Cunningham, Coates-Goshen, Ohio and Abbott.

Since 1909 to date new cars put on the market include:

Stutz (1911), Chevrolet (1912), Grand, Chandler, Saxon and Scripps-Booth (1913), Dodge and Dort (1914), Owen Magnetic (1915), Drexel and Elgin (1916). Other automobiles in the field are the Maibohm, Allen, Ben-Hur, Crow-Elkhart, Harroun, Lexington and Madison.

A table giving a complete list of automobiles is printed elsewhere in this volume.

The earlier manufacturers of motor cars included many who had been engaged in manufacturing bicycles, and following them was a group that had successfully manufactured wagons and carriages. Still another set of manufacturers were machinery men.

In the list of names of automobile companies which have been organized during the period of the industry's development, there are some which have gone out of business, but not many.

The industry, generally speaking, has had comparatively few complete failures. Mortality has been lower with it than with many other business enterprises.

This is chiefly due to the intelligence which the manufacturers brought to the business, plus the demand which sprang up for the automobile as soon as the people, instructed with great and liberal space by the press, realized it was the vehicle that could give what they wanted. Never was the value of a concerted campaign of education better demonstrated.

That unusually intelligent study of the subject of suiting the popular desire was given by manufacturers is evidenced in many ways, but in none that is so typical as was the standardization of motor cars.

At one stage of the industry its very life was threatened by a lack of uniformity in the mechanical construction of the various types of the automobile.

The big idea that has made Henry Ford's millions was a combination one. It was the building of a motor and car combined which could be constructed at a cost that would command large quantity production. This conception by Ford, alone, simple though it was, proclaims him the genius he undoubtedly is.

The purchase of cars between 1898, when sales first began to be made, and 1903, when Ford put out his car, was practically confined to people of wealth and leisure. It required both to own and operate an automobile. Men bought them at a cost of $3,000 to $12,000 each. Purchasers were exhilarated by auto-intoxication—with little thought of the practical uses the invention could be put to. Snobbishness, social impression and display of superior wealth were back of many purchases.

But for the manufacturers' quick recognition that the future of the automobile did not rest with the rich, that to be a great money-making industry, they must make automobiles for the mass and not for the class, the business would probably today be no further advanced than it was fifteen years ago. A parallel of what might have been may be found in yachting or motor boating—two methods of deriving pleasure and speed which are confined to the rich, largely because prohibitive in cost to the mass.

Popularization of the automobile demanded standardization. Automobilization of the nation would never be accomplished if the hundreds of manufacturers that sprang up produced hundreds of different cars with different sizes of parts, and different standards, requiring owners of cars with which something had gone wrong, to wait indefinitely for a particular device used by a certain company.

Early owners of cars learned by bitter experience what it meant to have a screw loose or a tire put out of business in a town where the supply stores did not sell that particular screw or that particular tire. The spread of distance, annihilated by the auto, was threatened by difficulties such as these.

High maintenance and repair costs ate up many an automobile buyer in the early days of the craze. It wasn't the original cost, although that was high enough; it was the upkeep.

Men of real ability—competent business men and expert engineers—got into the business, fortunately, largely for the rewards it promised, and by standardization and systematization brought the cost production down.

Getting the Price of Automobiles Down.

The engineers banded together and studied standards of hard steel, screw threads and wheel rims. The manufacturers, preserving open minds, co-operated, and today automobiles are the most interchangeable of all assembled mechanisms.

But for this the farmer, the moderate salaried city man, the mechanic and the small tradesman would not today be consumers of motor cars. But for this the average price for passenger cars, originally in 1900 around $3,000 and by 1911 reduced to $1,000, would never have been gotten down in 1916 to $605.

The average price of all motor vehicles, combining pleasure cars and trucks, was, in 1916, $636. The preponderance of passenger cars at the lower prices brought the average down, since the average price of motor trucks alone was about $1,800. For every motor truck sold, eighteen passenger cars were disposed of in 1916.

With standardization and the consequent lowering of cost, the automobile industry acquired a momentum that has carried production forward on a constantly ascending scale, as witness these figures of passenger cars alone:

Year No. of cars made

Year	No. of cars made
1909	80,000
1910	185,000
1911	200,000
1912	250,000
1915	842,249
1916	1,617,708

The manufacture of motor trucks almost doubled in one year. The number produced in 1915 was 50,366. In 1916 the number made was 92,130.

The above table, showing the rate of increase in passenger cars made in seven years, makes it clear that the greatest growth in the passenger car business has been since and including the year 1911.

That was the year in which the largest number of medium and low priced standardized cars with refinement of detail and added equipments, selling from $1,500 down to $500, was first put on the market. Ford almost doubled his output in that year. The next years, 1912 and 1913, also he more than doubled each year his output of the previous year. And in 1916 he made nearly one-third of all the passenger cars produced in the entire United States in that year.

Could anything demonstrate more conclusively than these facts, that if you have an article within the price of the mass of the people, it will sell, if the people want it? The one idea of Henry Ford—quantity sales—saved to the United States the premiership in automobile making. For other manufacturers adopted it, some radically, others in a modified form. Its influence was unquestioned in putting the price of motor cars at a figure at which a person happening to have less than the income of a millionaire could afford to buy one, so that when every one of the many values and benefits of the existence of the modern automobile is scheduled, let us, in giving credit for them, place the name of Ford at the head of the list.

When we have arrived at our destination, or have attained an object much desired, our satisfaction is such that we are in a forgiving mind and prone to forget the sacrifices we had to make, the difficulties we had to overcome, the strenuous work we had to do. The end justified the means, and we don't think long about the hardships in the means.

Preëminence of the United States in the motor field has not been gained without hardships, sacrifices and disappointments by those engaged in it, nor was it reached by the immediate and uninterrupted success of all companies organized to commercialize the invention.

While, as we have stated before, the number of final failures of companies was small compared with those in some other avenues of enterprise in the development stage, the number of individuals and corporations in the automobile business that started on the wrong road and found it impassable, was not small. But here again it was fortunate for humanity, reckoning the automobile as one of the greatest boons vouchsafed the human race, that the mechanical perfection of the automobile was reached at a date coincident with more enlightened thought, a liberalism of view and a clearer vision of the possibilities of the future by our men of business.

For automobile enterprises that took the wrong road and got mired in the mud of mechanical and management difficulties and financial complications were, most of them, lifted out of the slough by men who knew the right road and were better drivers. Had the automobile developed mechanically to near-perfection a score of years before it did, not only would the people as a mass not have been ready for it, but it is doubtful if business at that period had developed to the point of efficiency where it could recognize the possibilities latent in the motor car as a money-making machine. Where money is, the best brains go. Capital is timid. But brains and capital want only to be shown.

Some of the most successful motor cars and motor car companies of today were deeply mired in financial difficulties a decade ago, but were pried and towed out and made great successes by new brains and new capital administered by a new set of men.

Nor was the industry immune from the bane of all invention industries—the patent right. The man who gave it the most trouble was the man whose name is far up toward the head of the list of men who were responsible for the inventive ideas involved in the motive feature of the automobile—Selden.

He kept the industry in a ferment for ten years or more, whether designedly or not, through his patent, the mere existence of which tended toward restraining its development by discouraging inventive expansion, and ceasing to exercise the depressing effects of a wet blanket on automobile growth only when the influence of his patent was neutralized by an adverse court decision.

The earlier commercialism of the automobile was characterized by many extravagances in expansive plans, high financing and even recklessness, not only on the part of manufacturers, but buyers of automobiles as well.

In getting the price down to a figure which is not excessive, the manufacturers removed the cause which militated most against popularization of the invention and provided one of the reasons for opposition to it by many people. To pay the prices which originally prevailed, men mortgaged their homes and women sold their diamonds and went bankrupt on the upkeep of the car. Manufacturers expanded too lavishly, overcapitalized, and attempted great stockjobbing consolidations, while incompetent officers were paid excessive salaries, until conservative financiers entered a protest and the banks called a halt.

The abuses which were co-existent with one of the eras of the automobile's development caused the industry to be regarded by a class of the people as a luxurious outlaw and a menace to the well-being of the country.

Vice-President Fairbanks raised his voice to protest against the new manifestation of human nature's appetite for joy and comfort.

James A. Patten declared a Kansas City bank held fifty-two mortgages on as many automobiles, and that that sort of loaning was going to be stopped.

Certain banks blocked, as far as possible, loans for purchases of automobiles. A prominent banker as late as 1910 declared that the initial cost of automobiles to American users, being $250,000,000 a year, with as much more for upkeep and incidental expense, was equivalent in actual economic waste each year to twice the value of property destroyed in the San Francisco Earthquake.

A year after this statement was made, 1911, saw the dawn of the epoch of low priced cars, and the low priced car has reversed the condition from an economic waste, if such it was, to an economic gain, which it undoubtedly is.

Through all the storms of protest and criticisms, manufacturers went on their way, just as the automobile inventors had done under similar circumstances when men laughed and scoffed at them and called them crazy.

The depression of 1893 came too early to affect the automobile industry, but that of 1907 hit it at the time when it was by no means as strong as it was later; and yet, while in that year dozens of companies were bankrupted, and in 1910, fifty-two went out of business, it should be said that the great majority of them were not actually starters in the race. They were entrants that never toed the scratch. Their failure to make a start was due to lack of capital or inefficient organizers. A very large proportion of automobile companies that actually started in business have survived and are successful.

Names of automobile manufacturers who are prominent today were familiar names in the earlier stages of the industry, and more of the original automobile makers have survived than have fallen by the wayside.

Removing Obstacles to Automobile Production.

One objection the old philosopher has to the automobile is an objection that is strengthened by the fact that he does not own one. It is that the automobile contributes toward making the age one in which a really short time appears to be and is generally regarded as a long time. It destroys proportions as it annihilates space.

Seventeen years is a shorter time in the view of the philosopher of 60, accustomed to reviewing events in his past life half a century back, than it appears to a man of 34. It is just half the length of this young man's years. Time, as to duration, is thus comparative to different views.

Seventeen years is not long for a commercial industry to take the place which the automobile business now occupies in a country as great as this. It is a short time in which to build up a business representing the figures of two billion on the mark of the American dollar.

But this business, which has not been a business for even a score of years, did not arrive at its present estate without vicissitudes, and without strenuous work in removing obstacles in the way of its progress.

The seventeen years in which the industry made its record, saw the rise and the fall of the steamer type of car, the wresting of an Old Man of the Sea, in the form of a discouraging patent holder from the shoulders of the manufacturers, the electric car largely depopularized and the gasoline car established in wellnigh universal favor.

The procession of the more important earlier pioneers in the commercialization of the automobile started with the Pope Manufacturing Company at its head. In 1897 this company, which had successfully made bicycles, manufactured electric cars at Hartford, but was unable to find a market for them in the United States. An effort was made to get the Newport set to take them up, but the wealthy owners of Newport villas could not be induced to be even mildly interested.

So the Pope company decided to send them abroad, and shipped them on the steamer La Bourgogne. But this ship sank at sea and the cars were lost. The Pope company then made electric cabs, many of which appeared on the streets of New York in 1898 and 1899, and finally sold its electric vehicle business to the Columbia Automobile Company of New Jersey.

This corporation was formed by a party of capitalists headed by William C. Whitney of New York, and included P. A. B.

Widener of Philadelphia, A. F. Brady of Albany, and Thomas F. Ryan of New York. All were interested and actively engaged in street electric traction development in the East. Whitney, who was in public life as Secretary of the Navy under Cleveland, was a man of far vision in industrial possibilities, and recognized early in its development stage that the automobile had a future. He was as quick to see, also, that the gasoline motor drive was the coming means of propulsion, and he caused the Columbia Automobile Company, whose name was changed to the Electric Vehicle Company, to negotiate for and finally secure complete rights to the Selden patents for gasoline motors.

Having a sweeping license agreement with Selden, the Electric Vehicle Company undertook to enforce its rights, and one of the first concerns sued for infringement was the Winton Company, whose gasoline car, sold in 1898, was the first gasoline car disposed of by a manufacturer in this country. The United States Court upheld the patent, and nine of the then leading automobile manufacturers, finding they must pay royalties, formed an association under the title of the Association of Licensed Automobile Manufacturers.

For thirteen years thereafter, until 1911, gasoline automobile manufacture in the United States was under tribute to a royalty of from four-fifths of one per cent to $1\frac{1}{4}$ per cent of the retail price of all cars sold. The beneficiary of this license fee was the Electric Vehicle Company, which "split" the fees with Selden, and the Association of Licensed Automobile Manufacturers itself. The fees amounted to very large sums, and the licensees wriggled and squirmed; but the United States District Court having upheld the Selden patent, there was no way out, unless a deliverer appeared.

And such a deliverer did appear.

It was none other than Henry Ford.

For a pacifist, Henry Ford is about the greatest fighter the American industrial ranks have ever produced. His history has been a succession of fights—fights to make a motor that would go inside a hat box, fights to get anybody to believe in him and invest money with him, fights to convince people that nearly everybody would buy an automobile if the price was low enough, and finally the fiercest and most prolonged fight of all—the fight to break the Selden patent monopoly and free the industry from serfdom, give it free rein and relieve it of the incubus of tribute.

Ford had refused to join the Association of Licensed Automobile Manufacturers and had gone on making his engine and adapting it to a car which he put out, as has before been said, in 1903. The Electric Vehicle Company, which held the reins and was driving all the gasoline car makers except Ford, cracked its whip in Henry's direction and brought him up standing, and bristling as well.

In the suit for infringement against Ford the Electric Vehicle Company won in the lower United States court, but it reckoned without its Ford. That product of a strain of Irish-English fighting blood didn't consider he was whipped because one court decided against him, as all the other manufacturers, who submitted their necks meekly to the Selden patent yoke, had done.

He promptly appealed and fought the case like a wildcat up to the United States Circuit Court of Appeals, and through that tribunal, and with such success that, in 1911 this court reversed the finding of the lower court and gave the decision to Henry Ford.

The original suit in the lower court was begun against Ford in 1903, so that his fight against the first and only automobile "trust" was an eight year war.

But during it all, he never faltered in his activities in perfecting his car and making his elaborate preparations to build and market it. His confidence in his final victory was not affected in the slightest degree. He went on, pursuing his object with unruffled mien.

It must have been a trying brand of chagrin that the gasoline car manufacturers, who had tamely submitted to their first setback in the effort to slip the fetters of patent rights, had to wear around with them. They had looked askance at Ford. They feared he was likely to kill the automobile "game" by putting out a car that would make automobiling common, and put a damper on the purchase of the cars they made, by people who could afford to buy them. At best, he was calculated to be a disturbing element in the business—probably driving down prices to a point where there would be no profit in them.

And here he had been the savior of the automobile business.

Many men have written letters that have been their undoing. Selden had made an entry in a personal notebook or diary that brought about his downfall and the loosening of his grip on automobile manufacturing.

The ground on which the United States Circuit Court of Appeals decided for Ford and against the Selden patent was that the intent of the inventor had been to patent a motor designed after the type of a motor invented by Brayton of which the Ford motor was not an infringement, and not after the type of the gas engine of Otto the German, of which the Ford motor would have been an infringement, and that Selden had clearly disclosed this intent, as evidenced by a slurring entry in his diary regarding the four-cycle Otto engine, characterizing it as "another of those d—d Dutch engines."

The Otto engine for stationary purposes was in use before Selden filed his application for the patent, and if he did not intend the patent to cover an engine of that type he had no hold on the manufacturers who, with scarcely a single exception, were making automobiles, with motors patterned after the Otto type. These manufacturers could have done what Ford did—taken the case up and got the same decision, but they didn't do it, thereby making Henry Ford the emancipator of the automobile industry.

This delivery by Ford of automobile manufacturing from patent restraint and his quantity production idea, without any other of the many things he has done, would have made Henry Ford what he is—the most commanding figure in the automobile industry today.

There can be no doubt that the very existence of the Selden patent with the rights it conferred to tax every single automobile, was a deterrent to the growth of the business, because with the wiping out, through Ford's court victory, of the right of William C. Whitney's Electric Vehicle Company to take toll of all gasoline autocars produced, encouragement was given to capital to invest more largely in the business.

If, in the springtime, the season when the grass begins to sprout, you remove an old door that has lain flat on the grass all winter, the grass in the space covered by that door will literally spring up.

So when the lid—the Selden patent—was lifted from the automobile industry, it sprang to the front. The year 1911 was the epochal year in volume of production in the business. From that year dates the present era of automobile high production. It wasn't that many new companies entered the field. It was that those already in it expanded and increased their output. There was no longer an Old Man of the Sea, in the form of a tax on production, clinging to their necks and shoulders. The age of standardization had come, and the soundness of Ford's quantity production idea had been demonstrated. Thence on, the automobile industry had a clear course, if not in all cases easy sailing, and it has traversed it on a straight line, with a current of popular demand running strong in the direction it has been headed.

Gasoline Car in Popular Demand.

Pioneers in manufacturing gasoline cars during the period beginning at the time—1898—when the first gasoline car, a Winton, was sold, were Clarke Bros., makers of the Auto-car, E. R. Thomas whose name the Thomas Flier took, Stearns, Chalmers, Jeffery, Wilkinson, who designed the Franklin car, Olds who changed from steam to gasoline, Brush, Ford, Leland who produced the Cadillac, Haynes and Apperson. Many familiar cars came into the field later, or were developed and advertised by men who became identified with them at a later date. Although its manufacture was started in 1903, the Overland car, which ranks second to Ford in quantity production, did not become the factor in the industry it is today until John North Willys, a salesman, became identified with it and gave it its remarkable vogue through his personality and spectacular salesmanship.

The gasoline car was struggling to perfection when the electric and steam types of cars were reasonably well established on the market.

In 1896, New England saw its first motor race of electric cars. The names of make or makers of electric cars familiar from that date on include those of Riker, Pope, Waverley, Baker, Woods, Barrows, Studebaker, whose first cars were electric, Columbus Buggy, Rauch & Lang, Detroit, Ohio and Anderson.

But the electric car industry never has reached the proportions of the gasoline car industry. It has never advertised in the lavish manner adopted by gasoline car makers. It has not entered races to the extent its gasoline competitors have. It adopted conservative methods which have given it a slow growth. It is only within the last five years that shaft drives have been perfected in electric car construction, while producing controllers that would not arc, whatever the provocation, have been matters of slow evolution.

But that the electric car is a perfectly balanced piece of mechanism and the one type of the automobile with the least fits and starts, is conceded, and this superiority will doubtless enable the electric type to make up in the future in the motor truck field what it has lost to the gasoline type in the passenger field.

If the passenger automobile has not reached the length of its use and consumption, and it unquestionably has not, what shall be said of the freight automobile, the industry in which is yet in embryo?

The greatest future field for the automobile is without doubt in this direction, as is evidenced by numberless indications.

The increase in motor trucks made in 1916 over 1915 was within less than 8,000 of being double the number of the previous year. The number produced in 1916 was 92,130, against 50,369 in 1915, with an increase in retail value of $40,000,000. A business that nearly doubles in product while showing an increase in total sales of only 33⅓ per cent, as the automobile truck business does, is seen by analysis to be getting the price of its units down, and that is the surest means in commercial production to insure increased consumption.

Perfected devices are operating in the motor truck field as they did in the passenger car field to lower cost, and the lower the cost of motor trucks is gotten down, the more people will buy them.

The field of the motor truck's usefulness is ever widening. The European war has demonstrated many directions in which it can be utilized, while its adaptation to the country is as feasible and economical as its adoption by the city. Its use by

National, state and city governmental departments is growing rapidly, and the best evidence exists of its superior economy to the horse for many purposes. And when the high wave of motor truck use rolls in,118 the electric type will be found riding on its crest. Already there are upwards of 50,000 electric trucks alone in use.

The electric passenger car, while far behind the gasoline car in the race of automobiles, is distinctly in the lead of the steam type. Never was the biblical saying, "And the first shall be last," truer than of the steam automobile. First to arrive at the starting line, it was distanced early in the quarter stretch. The first steam car in the United States was sold in 1889, the first electric in 1892 and the first gasoline in 1898. And though it had a start over the gasoline car of nine years, it was never able seriously to compete with it, and 1905 saw only one large manufacturer left in the steam car industry.

At one time, about 1900, it looked as though steam and gasoline cars were running neck and neck in popular favor, and the names of Riker, White, C. E. Whitney and Stanley were as well known almost as those of Ford, Chalmers and a score of gasoline car makers are known today, but the contest was a short one.

The gasoline car forged ahead. Its success discouraged the steam car makers, most of whom changed from steam car to gasoline car manufacturing, and the business of steam car making narrowed down to two manufacturers—Stanley and White. Finally, in 1911, White gave up making steam cars and devoted his facilities to gasoline cars only, leaving Stanley to share only with Doble in the steam field.

The reason why the car buying public gave enthusiastic patronage to gasoline cars and scant encouragement to steam cars was that the use of the steam car requires more mechanical knowledge than does that of the gasoline car, and the work of making repairs is more complicated. The man of today wants to do a thing in the easiest way. His education, through the conveniences supplied in modern life, is all along the line of short cuts to anywhere and anything. "Why work when you don't have to," is his motto, and he has never been able to see why he should take the time to become a proficient mechanic to give himself pleasure, when he can buy

A GASOLINE CAR AND ESCAPE DOING SO—AND MUCH WORK IN RUNNING HIS CAR AND REPAIRING IT, AS WELL.

THE STEAM AUTOMOBILE REACHED THE ZENITH OF ITS VOGUE PRIOR TO 1905. BEGINNING WITH THAT YEAR, ITS USE DECLINED AND THAT OF GASOLINE CARS INCREASED. THE GASOLINE TYPE IS NOW ALMOST UNIVERSAL IN PASSENGER AUTOMOBILES, AND THE FACT THAT THE POWER UNITS IN THE OPERATION OF THE GASOLINE MOTOR ARE MORE ECONOMICAL THAN EITHER ELECTRICITY OR STEAM, HAS ITS BEARING ON THEIR GENERAL POPULARITY.

AUTOMOBILE DEMAND MADE ACCESSORIES NECESSARY.

A HISTORY OF THE COMMERCIALIZING OF THE AUTOMOBILE WHICH DOES NOT MAKE MENTION OF THE MANNER IN WHICH THE DEVELOPMENT OF THE INDUSTRY CALLED INTO BEING AN ALMOST ENDLESS LIST OF INCIDENTAL AND ACCESSORY PRODUCTS, IS NOT COMPLETE.

THE PRODUCTION OF THE FINISHED AUTOMOBILE INVOLVES A MULTIPLICITY OF UNITS, AND AS NO AUTOMOBILE MANUFACTURER MAKES ALL OF THESE, BUT DEPENDS ON INDEPENDENT FACTORIES FOR CERTAIN OF THEM, THERE HAS BEEN A MULTIPLICATION OF ENTERPRISES SUPPLYING PRODUCTS ENTERING IN THE CONSTRUCTION OF AUTOMOBILES, WHOSE DEVELOPMENT AND FINANCIAL SUCCESS HAVE KEPT PACE WITH THOSE OF THE AUTOMOBILE ITSELF.

FOREMOST IN THE LIST OF ACCESSORIES FOR THE AUTOMOBILE ARE TIRES, AND THE INDUSTRY IN THIS PRODUCT IS OF VAST PROPORTIONS. THE PRODUCTION OF AUTOMOBILES—PASSENGER AND FREIGHT—HAVING BEEN 1,617,708 IN 1916, AND THE MANUFACTURERS HAVING DELIVERED EACH OF THESE VEHICLES COMPLETE WITH A SET OF FOUR TIRES, THE NUMBER OF TIRES REQUIRED FOR 1916 SALES OF AUTOMOBILES ALONE WAS 6,470,832.

BUT THE TIRES PUT OUT WITH NEW AUTOMOBILES FORM ONLY A SLIGHT PROPORTION OF THE TOTAL TIRES SOLD BY TIRE COMPANIES. IT IS STATED THAT EACH OF THE OVER THREE MILLION CARS IN USE IN THE UNITED STATES CONSUMES AN AVERAGE OF EIGHT TIRES A YEAR, SO THAT AUTOMOBILE BUYERS ARE PURCHASERS OF PROBABLY 20,000,000 TIRES A YEAR.

THE PNEUMATIC TIRE WAS ONE OF THE GREATEST FACTORS IN GIVING THE AUTOMOBILE BUSINESS ITS IMPETUS. CHARLES GOODYEAR, IN A BROAD SENSE, LAID THE FOUNDATION FOR POPULARIZING THE AUTOMOBILE, WHEN, BY ACCIDENTALLY DROPPING RUBBER ON A STOVE, HE DISCOVERED THE PRINCIPLE OF VULCANIZATION.

The development of the automobile was retarded for years, because, while iron shod horses, it would not successfully shoe automobile wheels. The greatest obstacle to the mechanical perfection, as well as to the development of the automobile by general adoption, were road shock to the automobile and mutilation by the automobile of the roads.

The pneumatic tire removed both obstacles simultaneously.

The pneumatic tire was invented by an Englishman named Thompson, who patented it in 1845. Dunlop, an Irishman, was the pioneer manufacturer in 1888, and Michelin of France first applied it to the automobile.

The manufacture of body parts is obviously a tremendous industry, and while the body is a prime essential to the automobile, it was a part that existed in horse drawn vehicles, and, therefore, did not play the part that the pneumatic tire did in accelerating auto development.

Comparable in importance to the tire was the nonskid chain, the invention of Parsons, an English engineer, who patented it in 1903. As the pneumatic tire enabled the automobile to be used more successfully and in larger numbers in good weather, so the nonskid chain enabled it to be used in bad weather. Prior to its adoption automobiles were used to only a limited extent in wet or slippery weather. Its adoption is credited with having added one month a year to the possible use of every automobile, a result which would naturally increase the number of automobiles used, through making them more efficient, and by decreasing the life of a car through added use.

Next in importance in extending the field of purchasers of automobiles was the self-starter, the invention of Coleman, who, though little known to the public, is the inventor of so many things in electrical use as to be comparable to Edison.

The electric self-starter is credited with creating a million automobile buyers, a large proportionof whom are women, and with having added nearly 15 per cent to the service of the motor car.

Other aids to the successful commercialization of the automobile are solid tires, invented by Grant in 1896; the demountable rim, invented by Perlman in 1906; sliding transmission, the invention of Dyer; the nonskid tread, and

CHAMBERED SPARK PLUGS, THE LATTER INVENTED BY CANFIELD IN 1898. OF MINOR IMPROVEMENTS, OF WHICH THERE HAVE BEEN SCORES, THE MOST NOTABLE WERE THOSE OF SIDE DOORS, INTRODUCED BY MARMON IN 1902; TOPS TO BODIES, INTRODUCED IN 1903; SPEEDOMETER, GASOLINE PRESSURE SYSTEM, CARBURETOR, SHOCK ABSORBER, ELECTRIC LIGHTING AND OIL GAUGE.

THE EVOLUTION OF THE AUTOMOBILE HAS BEEN FACILITATED BY EVERY IMPROVEMENT WHICH MAKES IT EASIER OF OPERATION, AND THE SALE OF MOTOR CARS HAS BEEN INCREASED BY THEM.

THE MORE ONE REVIEWS THE ADVANCE MADE BY THE AUTOMOBILE DURING THE SEVENTEEN YEARS OF ITS COMMERCIALIZATION, THE MORE ONE CAN APPRECIATE THE FEVERISHNESS CHARACTERIZING ITS PRODUCTION, WHICH CAN BE SEEN AND FELT BY ANYONE WHO VISITS THE AUTOMOBILE MANUFACTURING SECTIONS OF DETROIT, CLEVELAND, INDIANAPOLIS OR TOLEDO. THE DEMAND IS SO GREAT FOR AUTOMOBILES, AND THEY ARE BEING BOUGHT IN SUCH NUMBERS, THAT THE FACTORIES PRODUCING THEM WORK AT A SPEED AND UNDER A PRESSURE SUCH AS ARE PARALLELED IN OUR INDUSTRIALISM ONLY IN MUNITIONS OF WAR PLANTS. BUSY ARE THE CITIES WHERE AUTOMOBILE MANUFACTURING FORMS AN IMPORTANT INDUSTRY, AND BUSY THEY ARE LIKELY TO CONTINUE FOR YEARS TO COME, FOR AS A COMMERCIAL INDUSTRY THE BUSINESS OF MAKING AND SELLING AUTOMOBILES HAS NOT YET EVEN APPROACHED HIGH WATER MARK, IN THE OPINION OF THOSE BEST QUALIFIED TO JUDGE.

THE COUNTRY DISTRICTS HAVE YET TO BE HEARD FROM IN LOUDER TONES. THE POSSIBILITIES OF THE AUTOMOBILE IN THE COUNTRY, FROM A COMMERCIAL STANDPOINT, CONSTITUTE A FASCINATING SUBJECT FOR SPECULATION. ALTHOUGH THERE ARE OVER 6,000,000 FARM FAMILIES, ONLY 300,000 AUTOMOBILES WERE BOUGHT BY THEM IN 1916, INDICATING THAT THE RURAL ELEMENT SO FAR HAS NOT REALLY BEGUN TO TAKE HOLD OF THE AUTOMOBILE, BECAUSE THE NORMAL YEARLY SALES OF HORSE DRAWN VEHICLES, MOST OF WHICH WERE SOLD IN THE COUNTRY, PRIOR TO THE AUTOMOBILE'S ADOPTION, WERE OVER 1,000,000.

BY FAR THE GREATEST PROPORTION OF MOTOR DRIVEN VEHICLES BOUGHT IN THE COUNTRY ARE NOW PASSENGER VEHICLES. WHEN THE FARMER WAKES UP TO THE ECONOMIC SUPERIORITY OF THE MOTOR TRUCK AND MOTOR TRACTOR OVER THE HORSE, THE SALES OF OTHER FORMS THAN PASSENGER CARS IN THE COUNTRY WILL SCARCELY HAVE ANY BOUNDS. THEBEST GROUNDS FOR THIS BELIEF LIE IN THE FACT

That at present there are 5,000,000 horse drawn vehicles in use, against less than 300,000 motor trucks.

In this development of the motor freight vehicle in the rural districts, the matter of education will play its part, as it does in all evolution, but slowly, as it always does.

Just as the creation of farm products as a whole is being increased by educational means, so will the use of the motor wagon in place of the horse be increased by the farmers' information and knowledge of its advantages and saving.

When the farmers all learn and realize the full extent to which the use of the work automobile pays dividends on their labor, the commercializing of this vehicle will be in quantities probably exceeding those of the passenger car.

Co-operation's Part in the Automobile's Commercialization.

If there is any one idea more than another that is productive of results in development of large proportions, it would seem to be that represented by co-operation.

Individuals may make successes, but they are successes that are limited in their proportions.

The era of greatest material development in this country has been that in the period represented by the last quarter century. This is shown in the fact that our national wealth during that period has increased in a ratio unparalleled in any previous period of time.

Only a little reflection will show that same period to be that period in which the value and benefits of co-operation in business as a whole were realized and taken advantage of.

The principle of co-operation has been known since man learned to reason. It was applied in the building of the Tower of Babel and of the Pyramids. The foundation of it was a fact that man early in his evolution from the cave stage discovered—a simple fact plainly demonstrated, when primitive human beings found that one man could not lift a battering-ram, but that twenty men could make of it an instrument with terrifying powers of destruction.

An aspect of co-operation that was slow in imposing itself on the understanding of the business world was that if a man conceived a new idea, and he concealed it from others, he was not only depriving others of its benefits, but himself as well. In locking the door on his idea, he locked himself in. He did not reflect that the world rests on a foundation of co-operation; that nature is co-operative; that without co-ordination between the planets in space, the cosmic void would not continue to be occupied; that co-operation is the invisible chain linking together the world, sun, moon and stars, and without the binding twine of co-operation they would fall apart like the stalks from the sheaf when unbound.

Almost every valuable lesson might be learned from nature if we knew and fully understood her laws, and co-operation is one of the most potent of these laws. But it took man a long time to learn even the rudiments of this law of co-operation—that it supplied a force of a hundred horsepower where one horsepower was used before; that its moral influence was tremendous, and that it was to business what the steam radiator, internal combustion, or the electric storage battery was to the horseless carriage—a means of propulsion, a driving force, an agency of high power to produce progression.

There can be no question that the automobile industry had, in the era in which fate decreed it should make its debut, favorable conditions. Not only did this era happen to be the era of a better understanding of the science and value of advertising, but also the era in which a better understanding has been gained of the principle and value of co-operation.

Standardization in the automobile industry, as has been said herein, was an important factor in popularizing the motor car. But how could standardization have been brought about without co-operation?

Producers of automobiles, even, did not immediately adopt the real spirit and practice the true principle of co-operation. They formed an association with that purpose, but in the first meetings they approached the matter of genuine co-operation like a man walking in his bare feet on ground strewn with broken glass.

They kept up the practice of secretiveness; each man was afraid to "put the other man wise," still clinging to the ancient practice of hiding his light under a bushel—an impulse founded on that same semi-savage selfishness of

PRIMITIVE MAN WHICH IMPELLED HIM TO HUG TO HIS HAIRY BREAST THE SHIN BONE OF HIS "KILL," WHILE EYEING HIS FELLOW MAN WITH FEAR, HATRED AND DISTRUST.

GRADUALLY, THROUGH THE INFLUENCE OF MINDS MORE ORIGINAL, INDEPENDENT AND FAR SEEING, THE GLACIAL RESERVE WAS THAWED OUT, AND AUTOMOBILE PRODUCERS BEGAN PRACTICING CO-OPERATION IN ITS UNRESTRICTED, UNTRAMMELLED FORM.

WITH THE GENIAL, WARMING RAYS OF CO-OPERATION TURNED ON THE INDUSTRY, PROBLEMS OF VAST QUANTITY PRODUCTION AT REMARKABLY LOW COST, EASY AND RAPID ASSEMBLING, INEXPENSIVE MAINTENANCE, AND THE VEXATIOUS PROBLEMS OF FREIGHT MOVEMENTS TO BRING IN RAW MATERIAL AND TAKE OUT THE FINISHED PRODUCT FOR DISTRIBUTION, BECAME NO LONGER WORK, BUT FASCINATING PLAY. THUS DOES CO-OPERATION MAKE AN ELYSIUM OF THE WORKSHOP, TURN THE DARKNESS OF GLOOM INTO THE LIGHT OF DAY, AND GIVE GROUNDS FOR THE BELIEF THAT IF THE MILLENNIUM EVER COMES, CO-OPERATION WILL BE THE VEHICLE IT WILL BE TRANSPORTED IN.

AT ONE STAGE OF THE AMERICAN AUTOMOBILE INDUSTRY, THE EUROPEAN CARS DISPLAYED A STRENGTH AND STURDINESS SO SUPERIOR TO OURS THAT OUR MANUFACTURERS NEARLY DESPAIRED. THIS WAS ANOTHER CRISIS OF MANY IN THE INDUSTRY. BUT CO-OPERATION ENABLED THE CAUSE TO BE FOUND AND THE CRISIS TO BE MET. THE EUROPEAN MANUFACTURERS KNEW WHY THEIR CARS STOOD UP BETTER THAN OURS, BUT THEY WOULDN'T TELL. THIS WAS THE SAME OLD DOG-IN-THE-MANGER THAT HAS HELPED TO MAKE THE WORLD'S PROGRESS SLOW. SO OUR MANUFACTURERS, CO-OPERATING, WENT TO WORK AND FOUND OUT FOR THEMSELVES. TUNGSTEN, VANADIUM AND CHROMIUM SPELLED THE REASON. THE EUROPEANS HAD BEEN USING THESE AND OTHER ALLOYS, AND WITH SCIENTIFIC HEAT TREATMENT HAD BEEN PRODUCING A SPECIAL STEEL, AND KEEPING IT STRICTLY TO THEMSELVES.

TRUST THE PEEKING, INQUISITORIAL, PERSISTENT "YANKEE" TO FIND OUT WHEN HE ONCE GETS WELL STARTED ON THE SCENT. AND WHEN THERE ARE A LOT OF THEM, ALL PEERING AND PEEKING ABOUT, WHAT CHANCE HAS THE POOR EUROPEAN? BUT IT IS TO BE DOUBTED IF ONE "YANKEE" COULD HAVE "TUMBLED" TO CHROME STEEL. IT TOOK A COMBINATION OF THEM TO DO IT. THEY DIDN'T DISCOVER THE SECRET UNTIL THEY WERE BANDED TOGETHER BY CO-OPERATION.

CO-OPERATION CONTRIBUTED TO THE GENERAL ADOPTION BY THE MOTOR INDUSTRY OF THE AUTOMATIC MACHINING OF PARTS. WHAT THAT MEANT IN ECONOMIC PRODUCTION WAS THE SAVING OF MILLIONS

IN COST OF CONSTRUCTION, WHICH IN TURN GOT THE AUTOMOBILE DOWN TO THE LEVEL OF THE COMMON PEOPLE'S PRICE.

IN THE ADOPTION OF THE SYSTEM WHICH SUBSTITUTED THE "MACHINING" OF AUTOMOBILE PARTS FOR HAND PRODUCTION, THE INDUSTRY INSTITUTED SAVINGS OF TIME AND LABOR AND THEREFORE COST, ONE INSTANCE OF WHICH ILLUSTRATES THE ALMOST INCREDIBLE POTENTIALITIES IN SCIENTIFIC ECONOMY.

A BLOCK OF CYLINDERS, WHICH TAKES ELEVEN HOURS TO BORE BY HAND, IS BORED IN TWO HOURS BY AUTOMATIC MACHINERY.

WORLD YET TO LEARN THE LESSON OF ECONOMY.

WILL THE WORLD AS A WHOLE EVER LEARN THOROUGHLY THE LESSON OF WHAT THE SAVING OF TIME MEANS IN ITS EQUIVALENT OF MONEY? FULL REALIZATION OF THIS IS PRACTICALLY CONFINED IN THIS DAY AND GENERATION TO SOME MANUFACTURERS, AND TO MOST EFFICIENCY EXPERTS. BUT THE GREAT MASS DOES NOT ACUTELY SEE IT.

THE FARMER KNOWS THAT IF HE TAKES FOUR HOURS TO GO TO TOWN WHEN IT IS NOT NECESSARY, HE HAS LOST THE MONEY REPRESENTED BY FOUR HOURS' WORK. THAT IS PLAIN TO HIM, BUT IT DOES NOT STRIKE HIM THAT TAKING FOUR HOURS TO HAUL A LOAD OF GRAIN TO TOWN BY HORSES WHEN IT WOULD TAKE ONLY ONE HOUR TO DO IT BY MOTOR TRUCK IS THROWING MONEY AWAY, AND IS AN ECONOMIC WASTE ONLY IN ANOTHER FORM. NOR DOES HE QUICKLY SEE THAT A MOTOR TRUCK WILL PERFORM SERVICE MORE ECONOMICALLY THAN THE HORSE, INCLUDING CHEAPER COST OF MAINTENANCE.

HE ALSO APPEARS UNABLE TO GET THE SAME VIEWPOINT ON THE ECONOMIC LOSS BY BAD ROADS, THAT HE DOES OF WASTING FOUR HOURS TO GO NEEDLESSLY TO TOWN.

THE FARMER HAS LONG HAD DEMONSTRATION OF THE ECONOMIC SUPERIORITY OF THE MECHANICAL REAPER OVER THE HAND CRADLE, THAT OF THE MECHANICAL THRESHER OVER THE FLAIL, AND THAT OF THE DRILL OVER SOWING BY HAND. BUT HE IS SLOW TO SEE THAT THE MOTOR TRUCK IS SUPERIOR TO THE HORSE AND A FACTOR IN GREATER ECONOMY AS THE REAPER, THE THRESHER AND THE DRILL WERE SUPERIOR TO MAN, WHILE AT THE SAME TIME HIS LIBERATOR FROM THE HARDEST TYPES OF LABOR, AND AN ECONOMIC SAVING TO BOOT.

WHEN ALL FARMERS LEARN THE FULL FACTS OF THE SUPERIORITY OF MOTOR MECHANISM OVER HORSES, ONLY ONE INSTANCE OF WHICH IS THAT THEIR COST PER MILE HAULAGE IS $16 \frac{2}{3}$ CENTS, AGAINST $30 \frac{7}{10}$ CENTS FOR THE HORSE, A WIDER USE WILL RESULT. IT IS ONLY THE highly developed efficiency expert who yet can count a minute of time in its equivalent of cents, and an hour in its equivalent of dollars. The automobile industry has had the benefit of the highest quality of efficiency generalship.

Chalmers was making $70,000 a year with the National Cash Register Company when an automobile company secured him by promising more. Flanders was offered by Ford, in addition to his salary, a bonus of $20,000 if, in the first year of his administration, he would turn out 10,000 cars. By installing the first automatic machine tool system, which itself was mechanical co-operation, Flanders collected the bonus.

No industry, except perhaps oil or steel, has paid men such salaries, bonuses and commissions as has that of the automobile.

Co-operation by the automobile industry has been pursued in its public shows for seventeen years—the period of the industry's greatest strides—beginning with the first one in 1900 in Madison Square Garden, New York. The seventeenth annual auto show was that in New York and Chicago in January, 1917.

There are many lines of industrial production in which to this day the factors have not gotten together in co-operation, lines in which each producer is working alone, and it is noticeable in many of them that development is slow and advancement tardy.

The automobile makers early applied the principle of co-operation by formal association. They organized the National Association of Automobile Manufacturers to advertise automobiles at the first auto show in New York, and to "encourage general practices of mutual benefit," a statement of principles that is brief but sweeping.

Stimulating influences in the formation of this, one of the earliest, and one of the most comprehensive and sincere co-operative industrial associations, were the necessity for presenting a united front, which legislation adverse to the automobile created, and of popularizing and inspiring confidence in an innovation. Co-operation was further made imperative by the necessity for better roads. Had the roads of the United States been better than they were when the automobile first came into being, the industry might by now be

ABLE TO WRITE ITS ANNUAL PRODUCTION IN LARGER FIGURES THAN 1,600,000 CARS MADE IN 1916.

THAT THE AUTOMOBILE ASSOCIATIONS HAVE THE TRUE PRINCIPLE OF CO-OPERATION AND NOT THE SEMI-TRUE OR FALSE VARIETY, IS EVIDENCED BY THE FACT THAT THEIR CO-OPERATIVE EFFORTS HAVE BEEN FROM THE START FOR THE BENEFIT OF THE INDUSTRY AS A WHOLE AND NOT FOR THE BENEFIT OF MEMBERS OF THE ASSOCIATIONS ALONE. THEY HAVE ALWAYS ADMITTED TO THEIR COUNCILS ALL MANUFACTURERS, WHETHER ASSOCIATION MEMBERS OR NOT, AND CO-OPERATED ON A FREE AND FULL BASIS.

BROAD LIBERALISM HAS BEEN PRACTICED. THE MANY YOUNG MEN ENGAGED IN THE INDUSTRY HAVE BEEN CREDITED WITH THIS. COMING INTO THE BUSINESS ARENA AT A LATE DATE, THEY WERE NOT HANDICAPPED BY PREJUDICES AND HARDENING OF THE ARTERIES OF OPEN-MINDED THOUGHT. THEY BELIEVED IN THE PRINCIPLE OF "ONE FOR ALL, AND ALL FOR ONE," WHICH IS THE KEYNOTE OF CO-OPERATION.

AS THE WORLD HAS THESE MEN TO THANK FOR THE CONSTANTLY ENLARGING PLEASURES AND COMFORTS OF THE AUTOMOBILE, SO IT HAS THEM TO THANK FOR SUCH GOOD ROADS AS THERE ARE, FOR IT IS AS CERTAIN THAT AUTOMOBILES HAVE IMPROVED ROADS AS IT IS THAT AUTOMOBILES EXIST.

THE ORGANIZATION OF THE NATIONAL ASSOCIATION OF AUTOMOBILE MANUFACTURERS WAS FOLLOWED BY THAT OF THE CO-OPERATIVE ASSOCIATION OF LICENSED AUTOMOBILE OWNERS, ORGANIZED TO RESIST THE TIGHTENING OF THE CLASP OF THE LICENSOR OF THE SELDEN PATENT RIGHTS, AND BY THE SOCIETY OF AUTOMOBILE ENGINEERS, AND STILL LATER BY THE AMERICAN MOTOR CAR MANUFACTURERS ASSOCIATION. THE AUTOMOBILE BOARD OF TRADE FOLLOWED, AND TODAY THE TRADE ASSOCIATION IS THE NATIONAL AUTOMOBILE CHAMBER OF COMMERCE. FOSTERING TRADE, REFORMING ABUSES AND PROMOTING HARMONY, WERE STEADILY THE AIMS OF ALL THE ORGANIZATIONS, AND HOW WELL THEY HAVE DONE IT IS ATTESTED BY THE FACT THAT NO ASSOCIATION OF PRODUCERS HAS BETTER DEMONSTRATED AND MORE COMPLETELY JUSTIFIED THE VALUABLE PRINCIPLE OF TRUE CO-OPERATION.

STANDARDIZATION IN THE AUTOMOBILE BUSINESS HAS NEVER DISCOURAGED INDIVIDUALITY OF THE MANUFACTURERS IN THE ESSENTIALS OF FORM OR SPEED. IT WAS CONFINED TO THOSE DIRECTIONS WHERE APPEARANCE WAS NOT IMPORTANT. IT NEVER

Extended to bodies, stream lines or designs that would deprive a manufacturer of distinctions and selling points.

It is standardization of detail—uniformity of screws, locks, washers, spring and bearing parts, water connections, etc. Co-operation has been practiced intelligently, and the result has been that standardization favored economical manufacturing by creating a large demand, calling for quantities that fostered specialization in parts by manufacturers, with resulting low cost to the automobile maker. It also left him free to center his efforts, energy and capital on production in quantity, and himself get down the price of the finished automobile.

To the thinker, one of the most interesting features of the automobile industry is this example it has given to the world of efficiency and co-operation. We are not surprised at efficiency in the steel business or the oil business, because they are industries conducted practically by one man power; and if autocratic rule is not efficient, its last excuse for being might appear to have ceased to exist; but to find several hundred different manufacturers with divergent ambitions, ideals and interests benevolently engaged in co-operative competition, justifies, it would seem, that optimism which sees the world as growing better.

Certainly if "by their works ye shall know them," the progress made by the automobile industry in the short space of time it has played the star part on the industrial stage, has been the most splendid demonstration of the value in commercial industrialism of the tolerant, broad minded type of co-operation, coupled with efficiency. It is an example of the value of harmonious co-ordination of the differing efforts of man in advancing the material progress of the world, and in the case of the automobile industry, the best assurance of its continued advance as the moving force in the production of one of the greatest and most beneficial forms, not alone of transportation, but of mind culture, of healthful relaxation and of sane recreation.

CHAPTER IV.

AUTOMOBILE INDUSTRY AS AN INVESTMENT.

A dozen years ago dictionary publishers vied with one another to be the first to announce that new editions of their wordbooks contained the word "automobile."

Today the automobile industry is the fourth in magnitude—only three others that are larger.

Is your imagination equal to the task of forming a vivid picture of the tremendous activity that has been maintained to produce such results in so short a time?

Do you know of any other industry in which money could have been at work in as great a creative capacity? We will not say in a capacity to produce immediate profits, because so far the automobile industry has been largely in the building, in the creative state.

In 1899 we produced 3,700 automobiles, in this country. In 1915 we produced 842,249 cars, and in 1916 the production reached the unexpected number of 1,617,708 cars.

The value of the production in 1899 was $4,750,000, or about $1,283 a car. In 1916 the value was $972,336,400, an average of a little over $601 a car.

In 1916, also, we produced 92,130 commercial vehicles, valued at $157,000,000.

And this is not all. A comprehensive survey of the automobile industry will include the industries that the automobile has created, as manufacturing tires and accessories, and not to forget the enlarged market for gasoline and oil. As the jokesmiths have it, "It isn't the original cost, but the upkeep that counts."

For illustration, in the matter of tires, C. H. Williams, of the Goodyear Tire and Rubber Company, who is in a position to know, said that in 1916 the motorists of the United States took from their wheels and replaced some 9,000,000 tires, representing an expenditure in that year of about $300,000,000 for tires.

Any motorist can draw from his experience and compare the expense for tires with that for gasoline, and from these tire expense figures arrive at a reasonably accurate estimate of the tremendous amount of money that was used in 1916 in paying for gasoline to run automobiles.

By way of an interpolation, it may here be remarked that these tire figures show that there is one problem in the automobile industry that the engineers still have to solve, and that is to produce a wheel that will give satisfactory service without requiring a pneumatic rubber tire.

Little Original Capital Invested.

The remarkable thing about the automobile industry is that, in comparison with its present magnitude, there has been but little original capital invested in it. Today the industry represents a large investment, to be sure, but the bulk of it is made up of profits on the original small investment. Companies started with small original capitals, made money, and used some of it to enlarge plants and increase outputs, until today we have the gigantic institutions that some of these companies are.

The automobile industry has been and is one of the most convincing of modern proofs of the efficacy of the science of investment in operation.

During the first few years of experimenting, before the engineers produced a car that would run in a reasonably satisfactory manner, the industry offered investors only what might have been called the inventor's chance. These years were followed by a short period devoted to determining whether there was a market for the automobile.

During the time of experimenting and determining the market the average person could not be expected to become very enthusiastic over an investment in the industry. The average person has not clear vision in matters of this kind, and, lacking vision, he can not bring imagination to his aid.

And in those early days it required clear vision, good imagination and exceptional ability to reason from probability to fact to see the coming greatness of the automobile industry.

A few courageous men had this vision and this ability, and to them is due all credit for the establishing of the industry. In time others might have done it, but these men did it.

The making and marketing of automobiles that would run had but fairly begun when their popularity became so manifest that even an average person could see that the automobile industry was bound to become great and profitable.

Here, then, was an opportunity for scientific investment that was prodigious in possibilities.

Those who were intelligent enough to see it and progressive and courageous enough to avail themselves of it, and did so, today form another set of rich men.

Difficulty in Getting Capital.

The industry had great difficulty in getting capital. It was a new line, a new venture. Bankers and other "conservatives" could see nothing in it. They used their pet weapon of crying "speculation", "hazard", "risk", and so on, to keep people from investing in it, and, of course, did not invest in it themselves, or aid it in any way to get started.

But since the beginning of this century, when the automobile industry began growing, many of our people have, among many other things, built the great automobile industry into what it is, and made money. Not only this, but they will build it still greater, and make still more money.

Before we get through with this little analysis we will see that the automobile industry has not been more than half built thus far, and that the really big profits in it are yet to come, because so far much of the profits have been used in building the industry.

This industry is, therefore, a fertile field for scientific investment. Many companies that are quite well established need more capital to enlarge their activities, and there are comparatively new companies, and there will be more, having very good propositions in which the prudent investor can find excellent openings for putting a little money at work under advantageous conditions.

Dealers Put Up Their Own Money.

In speaking of the early financiering of the automobile industry, it would be unjust not to mention the aid that automobile dealers gave it. It is a fact that if dealers had not supported it in the way they did, it would not be where it is today.

Bankers who could have furnished the money and should have done so, did nothing. They were too "conservative" to recognize a new industry.

And so dealers stepped into the breach and became bankers to the industry.

In the days when the automobile manufacturer was confronted with the problem of getting money to pay for making cars for which he had or could get orders, some financiering genius devised the plan of giving the dealer exclusive territory for the sale of a car. In return the dealer placed an order for a certain number of cars to be delivered in small lots from month to month throughout the period of the agency.

Another consideration for this exclusive agency was that the dealer made a cash deposit on each car at the time of entering into the contract. The monthly shipments were then made C.O.D. for the balance due on the cars in each shipment.

The advance deposit enabled the manufacturer to make cars for the first shipment, and the collection on the shipment enabled him to make cars for the second shipment, and so on.

To manufacture and sell 1,617,708 cars in a year, as we did last year, appears like an impossible task, especially when we consider that only a negligible number was sold abroad.

The fact is that nearly all the manufacturers, especially those of popular cars, could have sold many more, had they had the facilities to make them.

In the midst of this condition some persons of narrow vision were wondering if there was a further market for cars, and were talking learnedly, as they thought, about the point of "saturation" having been reached.

In the meantime the big men in the industry were saying nothing. Instead of talking, they were laying their plans to make and sell twice as many cars in 1917 as in 1916.

Production Not Yet at Its Height.

There will come a time when the automobile industry will reach its height in production, but that time has not yet arrived, nor is it within calculable distance. Statisticians show us that there are over 5,000,000 rich people in this country. Many of these have, and more of them will want, each several cars, each of a different type and for a different purpose.

We have about 8,000,000 farms. Many farmers already have cars, but only a few compared with the many who will have them as soon as they have become convinced of their utilitarian value aside from pleasure. The farmer is a practical person and "must be shown." Give it time, and the automobile will prove itself to him.

Then we have several million persons who can not be classed among the rich, but who are in such reasonably comfortable circumstances that gradually they will become owners of popular priced cars.

And we must not forget the element that is "keeping up with Lizzie." Those of this class will also pay toll to the automobile industry.

And so far only between three and four million cars, including pleasure and commercial cars, are registered in this country.

Talk about the point of saturation. As yet it hasn't begun "casting its shadow before", much less having arrived.

Nor does it require prophetic vision to say at this time that the commercial car is destined in due time to surpass the pleasure car in number.

So far the commercial car has but fairly been tested. In 1915 we produced 50,369 commercial cars. In 1916 the number reached 92,130. From now on this branch of the industry is likely to increase more rapidly than did that of the pleasure car. It has already been proved that the commercial car has a possible larger field than has the pleasure car. A man may not feel that he can afford a pleasure car, but his business is such that a commercial car is profitable in it. Then again a man may have two or three pleasure cars, but in his business he may have use for two or three hundred commercial cars.

The business world is just beginning to realize the value of the commercial car. Not only does it cost less by the ton or trip to haul in a motor car than with horses, but more can be accomplished in the same time. The teamster may require six hours to make a trip that the motor car driver can make in less than an hour. Business men, great and small, will soon learn this, and the commercial car industry will grow accordingly. In fact, the demand is already ahead of the supply.

Tractor as a Promising Investment.

The tractor, a motor vehicle used to haul other vehicles or machinery, is a product that must also be classed as a branch of the automobile industry.

It has already been demonstrated that a good tractor is the lowest priced power that can be applied in the work of hauling tools or machinery that must move forward to do their work. Also that it is the only form of power with which a man can perform a prodigious amount of work in a day.

The tractor industry is, comparatively, in its infancy, but it has already assumed substantial proportions. It seems destined, in one form and another, to surpass the commercial car industry.

Recently one of the Ford Motor Company's leading engineers secured a patent on a device to convert an automobile into a tractor. This is done by substituting tractor wheels in place of the rear wheels of the automobile, and by reducing the power transmission gear so that the power of the motor will be used in pulling a load instead of giving speed. In other words, the car in the form of a tractor will be run very slow and the power saved in this way will be applied to pulling the load.

The wheels may be changed in a few minutes from pleasure to tractor, and from tractor to pleasure. With this device the farmer can have his car for pleasure and business trips, and when he gets ready to do farm work he can convert it into a tractor to do the work of half a dozen horses or more, and at very much less expense.

A valuable feature of this invention is that when a car becomes worn out for pleasure use it will still be as good as a new one to form a tractor with this device.

The device was thoroughly tested in all kinds of farm work throughout the season of 1916, and found to work perfectly and highly satisfactorily in every way.

The progress of the automobile industry has surprised some of our ablest economists, and it has given the long-faced, wiseacre, conservative financier a clean knock-out blow.

Having no precedent to guide them but human nature, the economists were unable to arrive at satisfactory conclusions in regard to the future of the industry and it ran away from their estimates.

Mr. J. George Frederick, of the New York Business Bourse, is perhaps in possession of more business facts, figures and data of all kinds than anyone else in this country, and is regarded as one of the highest authorities on business economics.

"Writing on this phase of the automobile industry in the October, 1915, number of the American Review of Reviews, Mr. Frederick said:

"With 2,000,000 automobile owners today, and every indication that the annual production will be more than the 703,000 produced this year, we face in plain facts a probable annual sale of over 1,000,000 automobiles every year, on an average, for the next five years at least. Until the automobile became popular there were about 1,000,000 carriages sold each year, and as these were undoubtedly sold mainly to rural and suburban population there is sound reason to believe that 2,000,000 automobiles per year is not an extravagant future prediction in the slightly more distant future."

Production Ran Away From Estimates.

Note that this was written at least three months before the close of the year 1915. The production of automobiles for that year, as we have seen, was 139,249 greater than that given by Mr. Frederick at the time he wrote.

The interesting thing in Mr. Frederick's prediction for the future is that the industry ran away from his estimate the first year after he made his prediction. He prophesied a production of 1,000,000 automobiles a year for the next five years. The following year, 1916, the production reached 1,617,708 cars. This is not against him, because the automobile industry is going forward by such leaps and bounds as to smash

ALL CONSERVATISM. HIS ESTIMATE BUT INDICATES THAT HIS FURTHER PREDICTION OF A PROBABLE PRODUCTION LATER OF 2,000,000 AUTOMOBILES A YEAR IS LIKELY TO BE MORE THAN FULFILLED.

IN THIS CONNECTION WE MUST TAKE INTO CONSIDERATION THAT THE EARLIER MADE CARS ARE BEGINNING TO WEAR OUT AND ARE BEING REPLACED BY NEW ONES.

ALSO THAT MANY PERSONS WHO BOUGHT SO-CALLED CHEAP CARS AT FIRST ARE DISCARDING THEM AND BUYING HIGHER PRICED NEW ONES.

THE TIME WILL COME, OF COURSE, WHEN THE SALE OF AUTOMOBILES TO NEW USERS WILL BEGIN TO DECREASE, BUT AS THESE SALES DECREASE THE SALES OF CARS TO TAKE THE PLACE OF OLD ONES WILL INCREASE. WHEN WE REACH THE TIME WHEN THE DECREASE OF THE ONE WILL EQUAL THE INCREASE OF THE OTHER WE WILL ARRIVE, APPROXIMATELY, AT THE POINT OF SATURATION THAT IS NOW WORRYING TIMID AND UNIMAGINATIVE PERSONS, AND NOT UNTIL THEN. EVERY FEATURE OF THE INDUSTRY INDICATES THAT WE HAVE NOT TRAVELLED MORE THAN HALF THE DISTANCE TO REACH THAT POINT. A MORE RATIONAL ESTIMATE IS THAT WE HAVE NOT TRAVELLED MUCH MORE THAN A FOURTH OF THE DISTANCE.

UNTIL WE REACH THAT POINT THE AUTOMOBILE INDUSTRY WILL BE IN THE FORMATIVE PERIOD, IN THE CREATIVE STATE. IT WILL BE GROWING LARGER AND LARGER, AND WILL BE EARNING MORE AND MORE FROM YEAR TO YEAR. BUT SOME OF THE EARNINGS WILL HAVE TO BE KEPT IN THE BUSINESS TO ACQUIRE ADDITIONAL EQUIPMENT AND AS A GREATER WORKING CAPITAL. BUT EARNINGS USED IN THIS WAY WILL BECOME ADDITIONAL ASSETS BACK OF AUTOMOBILE SECURITIES TO ENHANCE THEIR VALUES—TO CREATE ACCRETIVE VALUES.

WHEN THE SATURATION POINT IS FINALLY REACHED THE INDUSTRY WILL SETTLE DOWN TO BE ONE OF OUR MOST STABLE AND PROFITABLE MANUFACTURING LINES. NOT UNTIL THEN CAN THE TREMENDOUS PROFIT POSSIBILITIES IN IT BE DEFINITELY RECKONED.

EARLIER THE INVESTMENT, GREATER THE PROFITS.

THESE CONDITIONS BEING TRUE, IT SHOULD BE CLEAR THAT THE EARLIER AN INVESTMENT IS MADE IN THE INDUSTRY, THE GREATER WILL BE THE PROFITS. SPECTACULAR PROFITS WILL BE MADE BEFORE THE SATURATION POINT IS REACHED, AND TO GET ALL THE TREMENDOUS ACCRETIVE VALUES THAT ACCRUE IN THIS INDUSTRY THE INVESTMENT MUST BE MADE AT THE BEGINNING. THE FURTHER REMOVED FROM THE BEGINNING THE INVESTMENT IS MADE, THE MORE THE INVESTMENT

WILL COST AND THE LESSER WILL BE THE ACCRETIVE VALUE AS WELL AS THE INCOME ON THE INVESTMENT.

THIS IS A FUNDAMENTAL PRINCIPLE IN THE SCIENCE OF INVESTMENT.

WHEN THE SATURATION POINT IS REACHED MANUFACTURING AUTOMOBILES WILL SETTLE INTO AN INDUSTRY TO SUPPLY A DAILY NECESSITY. THERE WILL BE KEENER COMPETITION, THE PRICE OF CARS WILL BE LOWERED, AND THE PROFIT ON EACH WILL BE CORRESPONDINGLY LESS. THE INDUSTRY WILL BE SIMILAR TO THOSE OF MAKING HATS, PLOWS AND SHOES. IT WILL CARRY A SUBSTANTIAL PROFIT, BUT NOT A SPECTACULAR ONE AS NOW AND FOR MANY YEARS TO COME.

IT SEEMS, THEN, THAT, LARGE AS IT ALREADY IS, THE AUTOMOBILE INDUSTRY IS STILL IN ITS COMPARATIVE INFANCY—THAT IT HAS BEFORE IT A REASONABLE POSSIBILITY OF MORE THAN DOUBLING ITS PRESENT PROPORTIONS.

WHILE THERE ARE SEVERAL LARGE COMPANIES THAT WILL CONTINUE TO PRODUCE LARGE NUMBERS OF CARS EACH YEAR, IT IS NOT REASONABLE TO EXPECT THAT THESE COMPANIES WILL GROW FROM THIS TIME FORWARD AS THEY HAVE IN THE PAST.

THE EXPANSION OF THE INDUSTRY MAY RATHER BE LOOKED FOR IN YOUNGER AND SMALLER COMPANIES THAT WILL PUT OUT CARS TO MEET SOME PARTICULAR DEMAND.

THE INVESTOR IN THE INDUSTRY COULD SCARCELY BE SAID TO BE USING GOOD JUDGMENT IF HE UNDERTOOK TO HELP TO BUILD A COMPANY TO PUT OUT A CAR TO COMPETE WITH THE FORD CAR, FOR ILLUSTRATION; THAT IS, TO PUT OUT A CAR AT THE SAME PRICE AND THAT HE WOULD EXPECT THE PUBLIC TO BUY IN PREFERENCE TO THE FORD. IT MAY BE POSSIBLE THAT THE THING CAN BE DONE, BUT OFF HAND IT WOULD SEEM LIKE TAKING AN UNDUE CHANCE.

NOR IS A FORD PROPOSITION NECESSARY TO MAKE MONEY IN THE AUTOMOBILE INDUSTRY. THIS HAS BEEN DEMONSTRATED SUFFICIENTLY.

THE FORD CAR FILLS A PARTICULAR WANT OF MANY PEOPLE, BUT IN THE MAIN IT IS A BUILDER OF THE INDUSTRY AS APPLIED TO MORE ELABORATE AND HIGHER PRICED CARS. IT PREPARES A MARKET FOR OTHERS.

THE INVESTOR SHOULD SEEK TO GET INTO THE BUSINESS OF SUPPLYING THE DEMAND IN THAT MARKET.

CHAPTER V.

BENEFITS CONFERRED BY THE AUTOMOBILE.

That the automobile is one of the greatest boons to mankind will probably be admitted if all its benefits are fully understood.

The best teacher, it has been demonstrated, is one's own experience. In learning anything, the mind can never grasp the lesson it is told, with the same understanding it receives when the lesson is visualized by the eye.

Travel is acknowledged to be a good educator and to broaden the mind. This is because the eye sees and takes its own impressions, and does not depend on the impressions of others. Reading books of travel never instruct as does travelling itself.

The automobile is a healthful, exhilarating method of conveying people to persons, places and scenes that, before the automobile, they knew of only by hearsay, or by reading of them.

To estimate the extent to which this informs and instructs, we need only go back in memory to the isolated farm of a quarter of a century ago, and vision the limited horizon of the general knowledge at first hand of the farmer's family. Practically all the current knowledge they had was from reading, occasionally going to town or through visitors whose appearance was rare and made at long intervals. Seeing a new face in those days was a rarity.

The situation with a majority of the people in the country, before the automobile, was very much like the isolated farm family. It was like that of the entire country before the advent of the railroad.

No greater agencies for instruction in first hand knowledge than the railroad, the steamboat and the telephone had been introduced into civilization up to the time of the automobile. Now the motor car penetrates into places where the railroad, the steamboat, or even the telephone does not go.

Medium of Distribution of Knowledge.

Exchange of ideas between people is the life of wider knowledge, as the exchange of commodities is the life of world trade, and the automobile is the medium of exchanging information as money is a medium of exchange of commodities.

From time immemorial the greatest advancement of the human race has been made in groups; and the larger the groups, the higher the thought, and the more progressive the accomplishments have been. Big cities have surpassed small towns; small towns have been in advance of the country.

The reason for this is the greater opportunity afforded by numbers for the exchange of ideas and knowledge. The citizen of Rome or of Venice had the advantage of personal contact with numbers of citizens which the isolated rural Latin was denied, as the citizen of London, Paris, New York or Chicago has, before his own eyes, the thought and achievements of millions which the citizens of the country only hear of or read about.

The railroad first enabled the resident of the country to go to the small town, and the resident of the small town to go to the big city, and by personal contact gather the fruits of himself seeing the results of community or group work, which, before, had been monopolized by his city brother.

The automobile supplements this work of the railroad, and is even more widespread as it enables more frequent visits to be made, and penetrates regions the railroad does not reach. What was a frontier is now a suburb, while the suburb has become the downtown. The motor car has opened up the far reaches as nothing else has done.

Bigotry and prejudice are the fruits of ignorance. Where knowledge is they will not abide. In enabling people to acquire knowledge in their own way—the way that most impresses knowledge on them—the automobile is changing the thought and the habits of the denizens of the entire country. It is broadening the human mind, by giving it a solid foundation to work on.In the courts of law, among judges, lawyers and court attendants, it is notorious that no two witnesses ever testify exactly to the same set of facts. There is a variation of detail, and many times there has been such a

DIFFERENCE IN THE STATEMENT OF MATERIAL FACTS THAT THE DISPENSING OF EXACT JUSTICE HAS BEEN DEFEATED.

THIS CONDITION IS ASCRIBED TO THE FACT THAT FEW PEOPLE ARE TRAINED OBSERVERS. THE AUTOMOBILE IS CORRECTING THIS POPULAR DEFECT MORE THAN ANY OTHER ONE AGENCY—BY EDUCATION. IT IS EDUCATING PEOPLE TO EXACT OBSERVATION AND PRECISE KNOWLEDGE.

LIBERALIZING THE PEOPLE.

THE AUTOMOBILE IS A FACTOR IN CREATING OPEN MINDS. WHEN ONE TRAVELS EXTENSIVELY, NOTIONS AND PREJUDICES, BASED ON FALSE CONCEPTIONS, ARE AMENDED AND REVISED BY OBSERVANCE OF THE FACTS. IN THIS RESPECT THE AUTOMOBILE IS CONFERRING ON THE MASSES A BENEFIT WHICH, BEFORE ITS ADVENT, WAS CONFINED TO THE CLASSES. TIME WAS WHEN BROAD AND LIBERAL VIEWS WERE GENERALLY THE POSSESSION OF THE RICH, WHO ALONE COULD AFFORD TO INDULGE IN CONTACT WITH THEIR FELLOWS MANY MILES DISTANT. NOW THE AUTOMOBILE HAS AIDED IN MAKING BROADER VIEWS THE POSSESSION OF ANYBODY ABLE TO OWN A MOTOR CAR.

THE DEGREE IN WHICH THE SOCIAL LIFE OF THE WORLD HAS BEEN BENEFITED BY THE AUTOMOBILE IS THE FAVORITE THEME OF THE ENTHUSIAST ON THE AUTOMOBILE'S ADVANTAGE TO MANKIND. THIS PHASE OF THE AUTOMOBILE'S VALUE IS OF LESS IMPORTANCE THAN IS ITS BENEFIT IN INFORMING AND ENLARGING THE HORIZON OF THE MIND, BUT THE SOCIAL ADVANTAGES WHICH THE USE OF THE MOTOR CAR CONFERS ARE NOT TO BE UNDERRATED IN AN AGE WHEN THE MOST FAVORABLE MENTAL CONDITIONS ARE RECOGNIZED AS OF EQUAL IMPORTANCE TO A DESIRABLE PHYSICAL STATE.

THE HAPPINESS OF THE HUMAN RACE IS ADDED TO BY SOCIAL ENJOYMENT, AND THE AUTOMOBILE IS A MOST IMPORTANT LINK BETWEEN ISOLATION AND HUMAN INTERCOURSE. IT HAS RENDERED THE MEANS OF COMMUNICATION BETWEEN PEOPLE SO EASY AND PLEASANT THAT IT HAS ENCOURAGED AND INCREASED THEIR ASSOCIATION. EVERYBODY IS BROUGHT INTO GREATER ACCESSIBILITY TO EVERYBODY ELSE. THE FARMER WITH HIS FAMILY CAN VISIT HIS NEIGHBOR FARMER AND HIS FAMILY, MANY TIMES NOW TO ONCE FORMERLY.

WHAT WAS FORMERLY A LONG, ARDUOUS JOURNEY TAKEN AT THE EXPENSE OF PLEASURE AS WELL AS OF TIME, IS NOW AN EXHILARATING SPIN. THE FARMER'S WIFE AND DAUGHTERS CAN NOW GO TO TOWN MORE FREQUENTLY, AND MULTIPLY THE NUMBER OF THEIR VISITS TO friends. The automobile is the emancipator of the farm woman, bringing the scope of her activities out of the narrow circle of routine drudgery and monotony into the larger circle of inspiring activities.

Farm women's clubs have been given an impetus, through the fact that a woman may attend one in the afternoon with the assurance that by the use of the automobile she can return home in sufficient time to get dinner, which she could not do by the use of the horse.

Factor in Promoting Sociability.

The city man's wife in the suburbs can visit her friends oftener and more quickly, and the facility of speedy movement has given to suburbanites the benefit of the last acts at the theatre and the opera, whereas, before the automobile, they missed them in order to catch the last train.

The benefit of clergy has been immeasurably enhanced by the automobile, which, also, in addition to being itself an educational agent, has employed its speed and facilities in economizing time to increase the attendance in the schools. There are districts in the United States where children can not reach school in time without the use of the automobile.

What the automobile does for the city dweller, in enabling him to see the last act at the theatre or hear the last act of the opera, it does for the people of the farm in enabling them to spare the time to attend dances, sociables, entertainments and motion picture shows. Where formerly the time required to drive a horse made it impossible to spare the time, now time is scarcely a factor. The change must inevitably react to the advantage and benefit of humanity, if all work and no play makes Jack a dull boy.

The health advantage of the automobile is a subject on which there is a difference of opinion among medics. The ordinary layman, however, is disposed to cast his verdict in its favor in this respect also. Some physicians have expressed the opinion that the only respect in which the automobile is noticeably not a benefit is in the matter of health. Some of them think it does not give people enough exercise, and that at the rate its use is increasing it will not be long before man loses his ability to use his legs!

It would be a catastrophe indeed if the human race, through the automobile, reverted to the condition when primitive man, according to the Darwinian theory, swung by his hairy arms from tree limb to tree limb, using his feet only as a stabilizer. But nobody, unless a writer for a newspaper Sunday magazine section, is likely to maintain this seriously, and he only pretends to be serious.

Whatever man loses in disuse of his legs by riding, as compared with walking, may be said to be made up for by his use of them on levers of automobiles and in the other exercise or operation of a car. The fresh air and the sunlight—the great outdoors—are the big health factors in motoring, and man will go on taking a chance to experience these and other delights the automobile has to give.

As an Element in Eugenics.

And as still further offsetting the possibilities of decay of the human legs, which certain physicians predict, more constructive medical men have discovered that automobiling is becoming a factor in one phase of eugenics. It may not receive endorsement as a benefit in all eugenics as long as the charge can be made that since the use of the motor car the birthrate in Kansas has decreased, the discoverer accounting for this alleged fact on the theory that the expense of keeping an automobile discourages Kansans from assuming the expense of large families, but in one direction it is attempted to prove that the breed of certain Americans is being improved by the automobile, and in this way:

In certain parts of the country, particularly the Southeastern states close intermarriage is said to have been, in part, due to the inferior facilities for transportation, before the automobile came into use. Young men, it is said, courted and married their sweethearts, in the days when the buggy was king of local communication, within an average radius of five to ten miles, which accounted for people in those sections being cousins or otherwise related to one another.

Now that the automobile makes a thirty-mile or fifty-mile radius the equivalent of the five-mile or ten-mile buggy radius, the swains are seeking mates further afield, thus getting away from alliances with relatives, and there is a consequent decrease in the mixing of blood strains.

If this is true, tally one more in the score of benefits for the automobile, for it is the verdict of science that intermarriage between those of the same blood does not produce the best types, any more than does the interbreeding of other animals.

But in enumerating the benefits of the automobile its economic value easily comes next in importance to its service in imparting knowledge. Its health value may be a matter of difference of opinion, and its social benefits are comparative, but there can be no dispute about its educational value, and still less about its economic worth.

The factor time has taken on a new meaning and significance with the automobile's accomplishments in speed. Time is a vital element in the affairs of life. If the automobile's educational value can be expressed by the adage, "Seeing is believing", its economic value can be similarly expressed by the adage, "Time is money".

Part Played in Economics.

Time is likewise life under some circumstances, and because of this fact, the professional men who were first to make practical use of the automobile were physicians, commandeering it in behalf of life itself. How many lives have been saved by the automobile, which would have been lost through the slow going gig or phaeton, it is not possible to say, because there is, of course, no exact record, but the number is large. The mortality of today among people is greatly reduced from that of twenty years ago. The advance of science has, of course, brought this about, but the automobile is an important instrument of medical science, just as are the X-ray, the stethoscope and the pulmotor.

And the same cause—the element of time—which operated in the adoption of the automobile by the physician to the human body, has forced the veterinarian to use the automobile. This is irony—for the horse—and another nail in the equine coffin, but it is at the same time another demonstration of the automobile's superiority in efficiency over that animal.

The farmer demands that the veterinarian shall come in an auto to attend his sick horses or cattle, because he will not take the chance of death through delay. And this is scarcely gratitude—by the farmer to the horse—but it is economic pressure.

At every turn in the road of the automobile's advance, we see its economic value. We see in cities that the big department store is able to cut down its delivery expense from $990 to $350 a day by using a fleet of motor trucks instead of horse drawn wagons; that coal, ice, groceries, feed—practically all commodities in cities—can be delivered by motor trucks at a large saving of cost. Contractors, plumbers, plasterers, tinners, and craftsmen in substantially all lines, have figured it out and concluded that with the facilities of the automobile available, the horse is a distinct economic waste in their businesses.

The possibilities of similar economy by the farmer in the substitution of motor power for horse power have been indicated by many progressive farmers who have by experiments demonstrated that the cost of hauling and cultivating with motor wagons and machinery is less than by using horses, but the general economic saving by the use of the motor vehicle in hauling cannot get its fullest and conclusive demonstration until better roads are more numerous. Where roads are nearly perfect, results have shown the cost of horse hauling to be 30 cents a ton, against 14 cents a ton by motor truck, by the mile, figuring everything.

Influence in Getting Better Roads.

By far the direction in which the automobile has forced on conviction most strongly its economic potentialities, is in the matter of better roads. No greater tribute to the educational value of the automobile could have been paid than was paid to it by President Wilson when he signed the Federal Good Roads bill which puts $85,000,000 of national money against an equal amount by the states, into making better highways. It was the popular demand for better roads, following the general use of the automobile, that gave the country the improvements made in roads in the last fifteen years, and it was the demand from the same source for more of these improvements that resulted in the Federal Good Roads law.

Until the coming of the motor car the good roads issue possessed little vitality. For seventy-five years the Federal Government exercised a passive policy toward building permanent highways. Railroads pushed into virgin territory,

Cities sprang up along the right of way, but the rural arteries of travel remained in the same hopeless condition as when the pioneers waded through them afoot or on horseback.

With the first motor car came the first feeble impulse to the good roads movement. The first cars were sold to city men, who very quickly found out that where city pavements ended, there ended all hopes of further travel. Pneumatic tires availed nothing against trackless stretches of gumbo mud or corduroy roads. With the mechanical improvements in motor cars, the owners chafed at their limitations and demanded better state roads.

As a result of the agitation, many states have become active in promoting their own road systems, and quite a little has been accomplished in some localities; but the sum total of improved roads in the United States today is only 250,000 miles out of a total of 2,275,000 miles of roads. The Federal roads bill will give an impetus to state work on roads, and as its appropriation covers the next five years, 1922 should see a large increase in the miles of improved roads in the country.

The results in benefit to the agriculture of the country in a general system of good roads, will be most felt through the facility it will give the farmer in marketing his products. With the aid of the motor truck, the farmer may be able to meet, in many cases, the congestion-of-freight-by-railroad problem.

Adding to its other benefits, the automobile promises to be an element in the reduction of the high cost of living, and if it does aid in this it will be in two directions, first, as a freight carrier, and, second, by displacing the horse.

Facilitating the Passing of the Horse.

A horse, it is estimated, consumes each year the production of five acres of land. There are 21,000,000 horses in the United States, and therefore the fertility of 100,000,000 acres is enlisted annually in behalf of this animal. If this area, which is as great as Ohio, Indiana and Illinois combined, were released from this burden, and the products were human food, a very large addition would be made to the food stuffs of which the world is in such sore need. The elimination of the horse is progressing at a very rapid rate in cities, and the prediction is made that it will come to an end ultimately in the country, and that a horse in future will be only a pet or

AN ELEMENT IN SPORT. THOMAS A. EDISON HAS DECREED THE HORSE'S LIFE FOR PRACTICAL, GENERAL USE, TO BE ONLY TEN YEARS. THOSE WHO FORESEE HIS PASSING ON THE FARM SAY THAT AUTOMOBILE ENGINEERS ARE WORKING ON SMALL TRACTORS WHICH WILL BE PRACTICABLE IN THE CULTIVATION OF FARMS AS SMALL AS 60 ACRES, AND THAT THEY WILL ULTIMATELY BE GOTTEN DOWN TO A PRICE WHICH WILL NOT EXCEED THE ORIGINAL COST AND UPKEEP OF A HORSE, AND WILL DO MORE AND BETTER WORK IN THE FIELD.

THE LIST OF BENEFITS CONFERRED BY THE AUTOMOBILE IS INCOMPLETE, IF ITS USE IN WAR IS OMITTED. IT HAS BEEN SAID THAT IT SAVED FRANCE TWICE DURING ITS LATEST WAR. WHEN THE ONRUSH OF GERMANS IN 1914 BROUGHT THEM ALMOST WITHIN SIGHT OF PARIS, GENERAL GALLIENI, THEN GOVERNOR OF PARIS, RUSHED TROOPS BY THE THOUSANDS IN MOTOR VEHICLES TO THE AID OF GENERAL FOCH. THEY TURNED THE TIDE AND MADE POSSIBLE THE VICTORY OF THE MARNE.

MOTOR TRUCKS SAVED VERDUN. THE GERMAN ADVANCE HAD CUT THE FRENCH RAILWAY CONNECTIONS. HORSE DRAWN WAGONS NEVER COULD HAVE BROUGHT THE SUPPLIES. MOTOR TRUCKS DID. HAD THERE BEEN NO SUCH THINGS AS MOTOR TRUCKS, NOTHING, IT IS CLAIMED, COULD HAVE SAVED VERDUN.

IN WAR OR PEACE, THEN, THE AUTOMOBILE IS A FACTOR. AS AN AGENT IN THE ADVANCE OF CIVILIZATION IT OCCUPIES A SECURE PLACE. IT HAS DOUBLED THE POPULATION OF AT LEAST ONE CITY, AND HAS GIVEN NEW LIFE TO OTHERS.

IN FORCING GOOD ROADS IT HAS ENHANCED THE VALUE OF AGRICULTURAL LAND. IT IS A WELL SETTLED FACT THAT THE INCREASE IN SELLING PRICE OF FARM LANDS THROUGH GOOD MAIN MARKET ROADS IS FROM ONE TO THREE TIMES THE COST OF THE ROAD IMPROVEMENTS. THE LIKELIHOOD IS THAT WITH THE INCREASED USE OF THE AUTOMOBILE, BENEFITS FROM IT WILL MULTIPLY. THESE BENEFITS ARE, NATURALLY, NOT AS GREAT WITH ONLY THREE AND A HALF MILLION AUTOMOBILES IN USE AS WE CAN WELL IMAGINE THEY WOULD BE WITH THE USE OF THE MOTOR CAR PRACTICALLY UNIVERSAL FOR PASSENGER, HAULING AND FARM CULTIVATION PURPOSES.

MUCH BIGGER THINGS FOR THE AUTOMOBILE THAN IT HAS YET ACCOMPLISHED CAN BE SAFELY PREDICTED.

CHAPTER VI.

REPORT ON AUTOMOBILES, AUTOMOBILE ACCESSORIES AND TIRE MANUFACTURERS' SECURITIES FROM A FINANCIAL AND INVESTMENT STANDPOINT.
COMPILED SPECIALLY FOR USE IN THIS BOOK BY THE BUSINESS BOURSE INTERNATIONAL, INC. NEW YORK CITY.

(1) Economic history and its relation to stock trading in the automobile industry.

(2) Securities of companies traded in on New York Stock Exchange.

   (a) Names of companies.

   (b) Amount of stocks and bonds outstanding.

   (c) Par value traded in during 1906-1909-1912-1916.

   (d) High and low prices—range of each class by chart.

   (e) Dividends or interest paid.

(3) Securities of companies traded in on New York Curb Market 1906-1909-1912-1916.

   (a) Names of companies 1906-1909-1912-1916.

   (b) Amount of stocks and bonds outstanding 1906-1909-1912-1916.

   (c) Number of shares traded in during 1906-1909-1912-1916.

   (d) High and low prices—range of each class by chart.

(4) Securities on various exchanges in other cities and data for 1916.

(5) Principal companies whose securities are not generally traded in.

(6) Some leading examples of prices and terms and promotion plans upon which securities were put out.

(7) Newer entrants into the security market.

(8) Security issues of tire companies.

(9) Some leading examples of appreciation or depreciation in value of such stocks since they were put out.

(10) General comparison with

    (a) Railroad securities.

    (b) Steel and iron.

    (c) General industrials.

    (d) Mining.

    (e) Chart illustrating above.

(11) Present trend of values of

    (a) Automobile securities.

    (b) Automobile accessory securities.

    (c) Tire securities.

(12) Possible future trend in automobile industry as a basis for the future outlook for 1917 on its securities.

ECONOMIC HISTORY AND ITS RELATION TO STOCK TRADING IN THE AUTOMOBILE INDUSTRY.

THAT IT MAY BE POSSIBLE TO COMPREHEND THE TENDENCIES AND PROBABLE TREND OF ACTIVITY IN THE MOTOR STOCK MARKET, IT WILL BE NECESSARY TO LOOK BACK AT ECONOMIC CONDITIONS WHICH PREVAILED AT THE TIME OF THE AUTOMOBILE'S INFANCY, AND AT THE CONDITIONS DURING VARIOUS PERIODS SINCE THEN.

NO INDUSTRY IN OUR TIMES HAS SHOWN SUCH PHENOMENAL GROWTH AND IN NO COUNTRY HAS ITS DEVELOPMENT BEEN SO MARKED OR REACHED SUCH PROPORTIONS AS IN OUR OWN.

IN THE EARLIEST STAGE OF THE INDUSTRY, THE AUTOMOBILE WAS ACCEPTED AS A FAD, AND IT HAS BEEN STATED THAT THE AMERICAN PEOPLE TOOK HOLD OF THE FAD AS AN INTOXICANT, PAYING AS HIGH AS FROM $6,000 TO $12,000 FOR A CAR, AND REVELED IN ALL THE NATURAL RESULTANT VICES OF EXTRAVAGANCE, SNOBBISHNESS, EXCESS AND CARELESSNESS. HOUSES WERE MORTGAGED AND RUIN WAS ACCOMPLISHED FOR MANY WHO PAID HIGH PRICES AND THEN COULD NOT STAND MAINTENANCE AND REPAIR COST.

THE RELATIVE EFFECT ON BUSINESS THEN BECAME APPARENT. BANKERS PROTESTED AND ENTERED COMPLAINT AGAINST THE AUTOMOBILE AS A DEGENERATING FACTOR IN LIFE. AUTOMOBILE MANUFACTURERS EXPANDED LAVISHLY, OVER-CAPITALIZED, UNDERTOOK TO EFFECT GREAT STOCK-JOBBING CONSOLIDATIONS, UNTIL CONSERVATIVE

FINANCIERS TOOK STEPS TO STOP THE HARMFUL WASTE AND INFLATION AND MANY BUBBLES BURST.

DURING THIS PERIOD, THEREFORE, STOCKS OF THE AUTOMOBILE GROUP WERE LOOKED UPON SKEPTICALLY, AND WERE SCARCELY KNOWN IN THE LEGITIMATE MARKET BEFORE 1912, WITH THE EXCEPTION OF A FEW SCATTERED STOCKS, SOME OF WHICH ARE NOW ALTOGETHER OUT OF EXISTENCE OR MERGED IN NEW COMPANIES.

WHILE STOCK TRADING DID NOT COME INTO GENERAL PROMINENCE UNTIL WITHIN THE LAST FIVE YEARS, IT IS AGREED THAT ECONOMIC CONDITIONS HAVE HAD A BIG INFLUENCE IN BRINGING ABOUT THIS RECOGNITION.

IN FURTHER CONSIDERING THE OUTLOOK IN THIS INDUSTRY, IT IS NECESSARY TO ANALYZE THE BUYING POWER OF THE POPULATION. THIS WILL HAVE A DECIDED EFFECT UPON STOCK ACTIVITY, WHICH THE REMARKABLE HISTORY OF THIS INDUSTRY HAS PLACED IN A CLASS ALMOST BY ITSELF.

THE PEOPLE OF THE COUNTRY NEVER BEFORE ENJOYED THE MONEY EARNING POSSIBILITIES NOW IN ORDER, BUT TO OFFSET THIS IS THE HIGH COST OF ALL ARTICLES GOING TO MAKE UP THE NECESSITIES AND LUXURIES OF OUR INCREASINGLY COMPLEX MODERN EXISTENCE.

IN 1906 THERE WERE REGISTERED (MOSTLY BY BUYERS OF AN EARNING CAPACITY OF $3,000 OR MORE) 48,000 AUTOMOBILES. SINCE THEN REGISTRATION HAS INCREASED 5,000 PER CENT, DUE TO THE CHANGES IN THE AVERAGE PRICE OF AUTOMOBILES. INVESTIGATION SHOWS THAT THE AVERAGE PRICE OF AN AUTOMOBILE IN 1907 WAS $2,123, WHILE IN 1916 IT DROPPED TO $820.

THE FOLLOWING CHART SHOWS THE CHANGES IN THE AVERAGE PRICE OF AUTOMOBILES SINCE 1904:

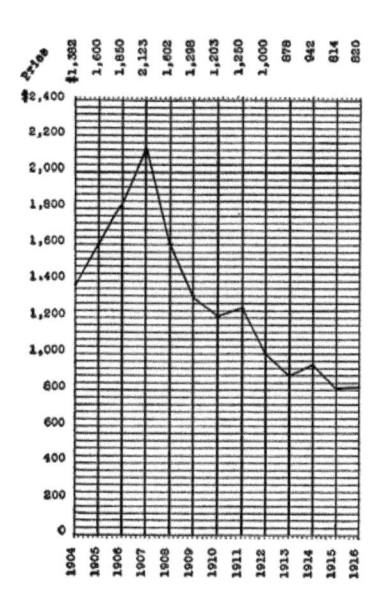

[Chart showing values from 1904 to 1916: $1,382, $1,600, $1,850, $2,123, $1,602, $1,298, $1,203, $1,250, $1,000, $878, $942, $814, $820]

In very few years this infant industry has grown to rank as one of the most important in this country, and it is plain to see how conclusively the industry's influence has produced an economic effect upon our national life. The farmer's life has been made more attractive. Cities have expanded into suburbs, thus affecting and influencing values on both urban and suburban real estate. Good highways are demanded. Thus it can be recognized the strong hold this industry has upon the nation at large, nor do present signs indicate that it will cease to grow.

Securities of Companies Traded in on New York Stock Exchange.

In making an analysis of this subject an expose along the following lines will disclose a definite basis upon which to make a survey of the history of past activity in the securities of a given industry, comparisons with other parallel industries, the present condition of markets for securities of these industries, and a forecast of what the general tendencies are likely to be.

The securities of the companies manufacturing automobiles, automobile accessories, and tires which have been traded in on the New York Stock Exchange for the years 1906, 1909, 1912 and 1916 are shown in the following tabulation, which gives an interesting exhibit from which it is readily seen how this

YOUNG GIANT OF MODERN INDUSTRY IS THE PRODUCT OF COMPARATIVELY RECENT GROWTH:

		1916		1912	
Name		High	Low	High	Low
Ajax Rubber Co.		89⅛	63	.....	.....
Chandler Motor Co.		131	88	.....	.....
General Motors Co.	(C)	850	405	42⅞	30
	(P)	128½	108	82¾	70¼
B. F. Goodrich Co.	(C)	80	57⅛	81	60¼
	(P)	116¾	110	109½	105
Kelly-Springfield Tire Co.	(C)	85¼	56	.....	.....
	(P)	101	95⅜	.....	.....
Lee Tire & Rubber Co.		56½	25⅛	.....	.....
Maxwell Motors	(C)	99	44	.....	.....
	(1-P)	93	65	.....	.....
	(2-P)	60⅞	32	.....	.....
Saxon Motors Co.		84¾	63⅞	.....	.....
Stutz Motor Co.		79½	48½	.....	.....
Studebaker Motor Co.	(C)	167	100⅛	49½	30
	(P)	114	108¼	98⅛	90½
U. S. Rubber Co.	(C)	70¾	47¾	67⅞	45¼
	(P)	115¼	106⅛	116	105⅝
		.....	.....	85½	75
White Motor Co.		59⅜	45	.....	.....
Willys-Overland Co.	(C)	81¼	34	.....	.....
	(P)	117	94	.....	.....
Rubber Goods Mfg. Co.		.....	.....	107	105

		1909		1906	
		High	Low	High	Low
Ajax Rubber Co.		.....	.....	.....	.....
Chandler Motor Co.		.....	.....	.....	.....
General Motors Co.	(C)	.....	.....	.....	.....
	(P)	.....	.....	.....	.....
B. F. Goodrich Co.	(C)	.....	.....	.....	.....
	(P)	.....	.....	.....	.....
Kelly-Springfield Tire Co.	(C)	.....	.....	.....	.....
	(P)	.....	.....	.....	.....
Lee Tire & Rubber Co.		.....	.....	.....	.....
Maxwell Motors	(C)	.....	.....	.....	.....
	(1-P)	.....	.....	.....	.....
	(2-P)	.....	.....	.....	.....
Saxon Motors Co.		.....	.....	.....	.....
Stutz Motor Co.		.....	.....	.....	.....
Studebaker Motor Co.	(C)	.....	.....	.....	.....
	(P)	.....	.....	.....	.....
U. S. Rubber Co.	(C)	57⅝	27	59½	38
	(P)	123½	98	115	104¾
		89½	67½	87½	75
White Motor Co.		.....	.....	.....	.....
Willys-Overland Co.	(C)	.....	.....	.....	.....
	(P)	.....	.....	.....	.....
Rubber Goods Mfg. Co.		105	105	43	42
		.....	.....	108½	100

Name	Dividends Paid	Bonds Outstanding	Sales in 1,000 1916	High 1916	Low 1916
Ajax Rubber Co.	1916—10 %	None	.....		.....
Chandler Motor Co.	1916— 7 %	None	.....		.....
General Motors Co.	(C) 1915—50 %				
	1916—25 %				
	1909—150 % Stk. Div.				
	(P) 1911 to 1916 (inc.)—7%	None			
B. P. Goodrich Co.	(C) 1912—2 %				
	1916—4 %				
	(P) 1912—3½%				
	1913 to 1916 (inc.)—7%	None			
Kelly-Springfield Tire Co.	(C) 1915— 6 %				
	1916—16 %	$270,000			
	(1-P) 1914—3%				
	1915-6 6 %				
Lee Tire & Rubber Co.	1916—$2.25 per share	None			
Maxwell Motors	(C) 1916—2½ %				

	(1-P)	1915—5 %	
		1916—7 %	
	(2-P)	1916—1½%	None
Saxon Motors Co.		1916— 3¼%	
Stutz Motor Co.		1916— $1.25 per share	None
Studebaker Motor Co.	(C)	1915— 5%	
		1916— 10%	
	(P)	1912 to 1916 (inc.)— 7%	None
U. S. Rubber Co.	(C)	1911— 1%	
		1912— 4%	
		1913— 5½%	
		1914— 6%	
		1915— 3%	$69,000,000— 5% ....
	(1-P)	1906-16 (inc.)— 8%	16,500,000—6% 1782 103½ 101¾
	(2-P)	1906-16 (inc.)— 6%	
White Motor Co.		1916— 5¼%	None
Willys-Overland Co.	(C)	1913— 11%	
		1914— 6%	
		1915— 11%	
		1916— 14%	

- 99 -

(P) 1913 to 1916 (inc.)— 7%		None
Rubber Goods Mfg. Co.		None

Name	Stocks Outstanding	Shares Traded in 1916	Shares Traded in 1912	1909	1906
Chalmers Motor Co.	$ 464,000	36,566	......	......	......
Chevrolet Motor Co.	23,909,000	660,550	......	......	......
Emerson Motor Co.	7,000,000	116,990	......	......	......
Falls Motor Co.		24,850	......	......	......
Grant Motor Co.	2,000,000	93,240	......	......	......
Preferred	1,000,000	....	......	......	......
Hupp Motor Co.	5,000,000	130,130	......	......	......
Preferred	1,500,000	....	......	......	......
Imperial Carbon Chaser Co.	1,000,000	637,850	......	......	......
Keystone Tire & Rubber Co.	1,000,000	137,200	......	......	......
Preferred	500,000	33,800	......	......	......
Mitchell Motor Co.	125,000	80,495	......	......	......
National Auto Corporation	61,865	......	......	......	......
Peerless Motor Co.	10,000,000	135,263	......	......	......
Pierce Arrow Motor Co.	250,000	52,300	......	......	......
Preferred	10,000,000	1,600	......	......	......
Republic Motor Truck Co.	62,500	20,870	......	......	......
Scripps Booth Co.	70,000	27,725	......	......	......
Smith Motor Truck Co.	10,000,000	39,500	......	......	......
Springfield Body Co.	1,750,000	26,481	......	......	......

Preferred	750,000	11,461	.....	....
Standard Motor Co.	1,800,000	47,490	.....	....
Stromberg Carburetor Co.	50,000	72,050	.....	....
United Motors	1,195,000	1,297,355	.....	....
Studebaker Co.	....	 16,973	.....	.....
Preferred	....	 4,717	.....	.....
U. S. Motors Co.	....	 53,393	.....	.....
Preferred	....	 54,433	.....	.....
Willys-Overland Co.	....	2,570 13,045	.....	.....
Preferred	....	4,350 11,045	.....	.....
Goodrich B. F. Co.	....	 40,846	.....	.....
Preferred	....	 32,211	.....	.....
General Motors Co.	....	....	 1,406	.....
Consolidated Rubber Tire Co.	....	....	.....	 2,843
Preferred	....	....	.....	 410
Ajax Rubber Tire Co.	....	102,065	.....	....
Alliance Rubber Tire Co.	....	14,400	.....	....
Preferred	....	3,200	.....	....
Electric Vehicle Co.	....	....	.....	 1,000
Preferred	....	....	.....	 3,705
American Motor Co.	....	24,500	.....	....
Pope Mfg. Co.	....	....	.....	 1,250
1st preferred	....	....	.....	 3,790
2nd preferred	....	....	.....	 5,450
Chandler Motor Co.	....	40,985	.....	....
Enger Motor Car Co.	....	7,456	.....	....
Essex Motor Co.	....	9,950	.....	....

Fisk Tire Co.	8,000,000	1,695
Fisher Body Corporation	200,000	20,130
Preferred	5,000,000	3,900
General Motor Co.	....	89,250
Preferred	....	13,416
Intereon Rubber Co.	....	76,848
International Motors Co.	....	8,441
Preferred	....	3,626
Kelly-Springfield	....	435
Kelsey Wheel	....	4,500
Lee Tire	....	41,175
Met. Motors Co.	....	2,825
Motor Products Co.	100,000	17,370
Perlman Rim	100,000	119,780
Princess Motor Co.	....	6,362
Republic Motor Truck Co. preferred	....	300
Saxon Motor Car Co.	....	102,226
Stutz Motor Co.	....	200,245
Times Sq. Auto Sup.	....	13,750
Universal Motor Co.	....	68,450
White Motor Co.	....	626,220

NEW YORK STOCK EXCHANGE.

THE RISE IN AVERAGE PRICE OF THE AUTOMOBILE SECURITIES TRADED IN ON THE NEW YORK STOCK EXCHANGE, AS SHOWN ON THE CHART, IS DUE TO THE GENERAL EXPANSION AND INCREASE OF THE AUTOMOBILE INDUSTRY WHICH WAS NATURALLY REFLECTED IN THE SECURITIES.

THE FOLLOWING CHART SHOWS AVERAGE PRICE OF ALL AUTOMOBILE AND AUTOMOBILE TIRE STOCKS TRADED IN ON THE NEW YORK STOCK EXCHANGE FOR YEARS 1906-9-12-16:

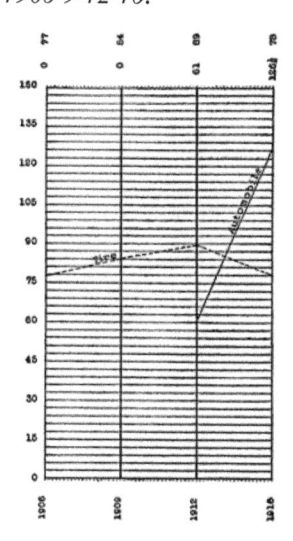

SECURITIES OF COMPANIES TRADED IN ON NEW YORK CURB MARKET.

THE SECURITIES OF COMPANIES MANUFACTURING AUTOMOBILES, AUTOMOBILE ACCESSORIES AND TIRES, WHICH WERE TRADED IN ON THE NEW YORK CURB DURING THE YEARS 1906, 1909, 1912 AND 1916 ARE SHOWN IN THE FOLLOWING TABULATION. SOME OF THESE CURB STOCKS HAVE GRADUATED TO THE BIG EXCHANGE.

Name	1916 High	Low	1912 High	Low
Chalmers Motor Co.	39½	33	.....	.....
Chevrolet Motor Co.	278	114	.....	.....
Emerson Motors Co.	4½	1¼	.....	.....
Falls Motor Co.	13	6½	.....	.....
Grant Motor Co.	14	7	.....	.....
Hupp Motor Co.	11¾	5⅛	.....	.....
Imperial Carbon Chaser Co.	53	12½	.....	.....

Keystone Tire & Rubber Co.	19⅝	11	.....	.....
Preferred	18¼	12	.....	.....
Mitchell Motor Co.	73½	51½	.....	.....
National Auto Corporation	44½	33	.....	.....
Peerless Motor Co.	31½	18	.....	.....
Pierce Arrow Motor Co.	65	42	.....	.....
Preferred	109	101	.....	.....
Republic Motor Truck Co.	74	54	.....	.....
Scripps Booth Co.	62	35	.....	.....
Smith Motor Truck Co.	6⅛	4½	.....	.....
Springfield Body Co.	55½	51	.....	.....
Preferred	139	101	.....	.....
Standard Motor Co.	10½	5⅞	.....	.....
Stromberg Carburetor Co.	45¼	38	.....	.....
United Motors Co.	94	42¾	.....	.....

	1909		1906	
	High	**Low**	**High**	**Low**
Chalmers Motor Co.	.....	.....	.....	.....
Chevrolet Motor Co.	.....	.....	.....	.....
Emerson Motors Co.	.....	.....	.....	.....
Falls Motor Co.	.....	.....	.....	.....
Grant Motor Co.	.....	.....	.....	.....
Hupp Motor Co.	.....	.....	.....	.....
Imperial Carbon Chaser Co.	.....	.....	.....	.....

Keystone Tire & Rubber Co.	.....	.....	.....	.....
Preferred	.....	.....	.....	.....
Mitchell Motor Co.	.....	.....	.....	.....
National Auto Corporation	.....	.....	.....	.....
Peerless Motor Co.	.....	.....	.....	.....
Pierce Arrow Motor Co.	.....	.....	.....	.....
Preferred	.....	.....	.....	.....
Republic Motor Truck Co.	.....	.....	.....	.....
Scripps Booth Co.	.....	.....	.....	.....
Smith Motor Truck Co.	.....	.....	.....	.....
Springfield Body Co.	.....	.....	.....	.....
Preferred	.....	.....	.....	.....
Standard Motor Co.	.....	.....	.....	.....
Stromberg Carburetor Co.	.....	.....	.....	.....
United Motors Co.	.....	.....	.....	.....

	1916		1912	
	High	**Low**	**High**	**Low**
Studebaker	.....	.....	59¼	34
Preferred	.....	.....	104	94
U. S. Motors Co.	.....	.....	9	1/16
Preferred	.....	.....	30½	¾
Willys-Overland Co.	47¼	41	72	67½
Preferred	106⅜	104½	101½	99
Goodrich, B. F. Co.	.....	.....	86½	70½

Preferred	.....	.....	109½	106¾
General Motors Co.	.....	.....	.....	.....
Rubber Tire Co.	.....	.....	.....	.....
Preferred	.....	.....	.....	.....
Ajax Rubber Tire Co.	73¼	63	.....	.....
Alliance Rubber Tire Co.	5¾	5	.....	.....
Preferred	8¾	8¼	.....	.....
Electric Vehicle Co.	.....	.....	.....	.....
Preferred	.....	.....	.....	.....
American Motor Co.	65½	60	.....	.....
Pope Mfg. Co.	.....	.....	.....	.....
1st preferred	.....	.....	.....	.....
2nd preferred	.....	.....	.....	.....
Chandler Motors	94	79	.....	.....
Enger Motor Car Co.	8	7⅜	.....	.....

	1909		1906	
	High	**Low**	**High**	**Low**
Studebaker	.....	.....	.....	.....
Preferred	.....	.....	.....	.....
U. S. Motors Co.	.....	.....	.....	.....
Preferred	.....	.....	.....	.....
Willys-Overland Co.	.....	.....	.....	.....
Preferred	.....	.....	.....	.....
Goodrich, B. F. Co.	.....	.....	.....	.....
Preferred	.....	.....	.....	.....
General Motors Co.	162¼	155	.....	.....
Rubber Tire Co.	4½	3	5⅝	2⅛

Preferred	23	18	16	12
Ajax Rubber Tire Co.	.....	.....	.....	.....
Alliance Rubber Tire Co.	.....	.....	.....	.....
Preferred	.....	.....	.....	.....
Electric Vehicle Co.	.....	18	13	.....
Preferred	.....	23	15	.....
American Motor Co.	.....	.....	.....	.....
Pope Mfg. Co.	.....	6	4	.....
1st preferred	.....	74	69	.....
2nd preferred	.....	21	14¾	.....
Chandler Motors	.....	.....	.....	.....
Enger Motor Car Co.	.....	.....	.....	.....

	189**1916**		**1912**	
	High	**Low**	**High**	**Low**
Essex Motor Co.	5⅛	3⅞	.....	.....
Fisk Tire Co.	168	115	.....	.....
Fisher Body Corporation	42½	35	.....	.....
Preferred	95½	93	.....	.....
General Motors Co.	175	117	.....	.....
Preferred	100	88	.....	.....
Intereon Rubber Co.	19	10	.....	.....
Inter. Motors Co.	25	3	.....	.....
Preferred	45	17	.....	.....
Kelly-Springfield	299	280	.....	.....
Kelsey Wheel	61	53	.....	.....
Lee Tire	66	44	.....	.....
Met. Motors	3¾	2¾	.....	.....

Motor Products	87	56	.....	.....
Perlman Rim	162½	111	.....	.....
Princess Motor Co.	1⅛	1	.....	.....
Republic Motor Truck Co. pfd.	98	98	.....	.....
Saxon Motor Oar Co.	87	60	.....	.....
Stutz Motor Co.	78	53⅜	.....	.....
Times Sq. Auto Sup.	41	28½	.....	.....
Universal Motor	9⅛	4	.....	.....
White Motor Co.	60	46	.....	.....

	1909		1906	
	High	**Low**	**High**	**Low**
Essex Motor Co.	.....	.....	.....	.....
Fisk Tire Co.	.....	.....	.....	.....
Fisher Body Corporation	.....	.....	.....	.....
Preferred	.....	.....	.....	.....
General Motors Co.	.....	.....	.....	.....
Preferred	.....	.....	.....	.....
Intereon Rubber Co.	.....	.....	.....	.....
Inter. Motors Co.	.....	.....	.....	.....
Preferred	.....	.....	.....	.....
Kelly-Springfield	.....	.....	.....	.....
Kelsey Wheel	.....	.....	.....	.....
Lee Tire	.....	.....	.....	.....
Met. Motors	.....	.....	.....	.....
Motor Products	.....	.....	.....	.....
Perlman Rim	.....	.....	.....	.....

Princess Motor Co. ....

Republic Motor Truck Co. pfd. ....

Saxon Motor Oar Co. ....

Stutz Motor Co. ....

Times Sq. Auto Sup. ....

Universal Motor ....

White Motor Co. ....

Name	Par Value	Stock Outstanding	—Number of Shares Traded in—			
			1916	1912	1909	1906
Ajax Rubber Co.	$ 50	$10,000,000	107,950	....	....	....
Chandler Motor Co.	100	7,000,000	291,640	....	....	....
General Motors Co.	100 (C)	14,985,200	43,215	55,436	....	....
	(P)	16,506,783	129,933	48,869	....	....
B. F. Goodrich Co.	100 (C)	60,000,000	604,055	65,169	....	....
	(P)	27,300,000	25,444	15,525	....	....
Kelly-Springfield Tire Co.	25 (C)	4,360,100	524,329	....	....	....
	(P)	3,593,000	5,335	....	....	....
	100 (2-P)	547,100	....	....	....	....
		(shares)				
Lee Tire & Rubber Co.	...	100,000	477,025			

Maxwell Motors	100 (C)	12,778,058	2,009,100			
	100 (P)	13,764,121	20,585			
	100 (2-P)	10,127,468	300,935			
Saxon Motors Co.	100	6,000,000	17,920			
		(shares)				
Stutz Motor Co.	...	73,301	116,900	....	....	....
Studebaker Motor Co.	100 (C)	30,000,000	3,045,440	50,652	....	....
	(P)	10,965,000	11,411	109,020	....	....
U. S. Rubber Co.	100 (C)	36,000,000	1,165,881	661,765	517,411	598,628
	100 (P)	59,692,100	69,147	78,734	199,512	123,611
	100 (2-P)	458,400	....	35,695	61,790	59,875
White Motor Co.	50	16,000,000	89,300	....	....	....
Willys-Overland Co.	25 (C)	38,655,710	1,852,745	....	....	....
	(P)	15,000,000	9,530	....	....	....
Rubber Goods Mfg. Co.	100	....	(C)	253	150	500
	100	....	(P)	....	....	625

CURB MARKET.

SOME OF THE BIG FLUCTUATIONS SHOWN IN THE CHARTS ARE ACCOUNTED FOR BY THE ABNORMAL IRREGULARITIES OF ONE OR TWO GIANTS OF THE INDUSTRY, WHOSE VOLUME OF TRADING PRODUCED A MARKED EFFECT UPON THE TOTALS TRADED IN, AND THEIR AVERAGE PRICES. INSTANCES LIKE UNITED STATES MOTORS COMPANY AND B. F.

Goodrich Company may be cited as examples. The accessory shares have seen a general rise since first traded in, in 1912.

The following chart shows average price of automobile, automobile tire and automobile accessory manufacturing stocks traded in on the New York Curb for 1906-9-12-16:

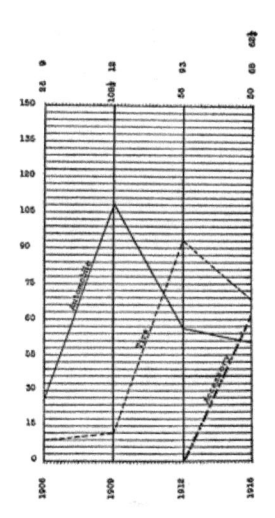

Securities on Various Exchanges in Other Cities and Data for 1916.

Securities traded in on various stock exchanges of other cities show very little activity or regularity.

Below is shown the trading in the great automobile center of the world.

Detroit.	1916	
	High	**Low**
Auto Body Co.	48½	32
Chalmers Motor	255	90
Chevrolet	277	171⅛
Continental Motors	42⅛	7½
Ford Motor Co. of Canada	415	275
General Motors	800	418
Preferred	127	112½

Maxwell Motors	95⅛	57⅝
Packard Motor	260	160
Preferred	104½	100¼
Paige-Detroit	57⅛	32
Reo Motor	47½	32¼
Reo Truck	45¼	23⅜
Studebaker	161⅛	120⅞

Cleveland shows greatest activity in the tire stock on account of its proximity to the great rubber center of Akron, Ohio.

1916

High Low

Firestone Tire & Rubber Co.	1,700	740
Goodrich Co.	78½	60⅜
Goodyear Tire & Rubber Co.	402	198
Portage Rubber Co.	183½	62½
Republic Rubber Co.	145	128½
Swinehart Tire & Rubber Co.	110	79
White Motor Co.	60	47¼

Principal Companies Whose Securities Are Not Generally Traded In.

Until the past two or three years, motor and motor accessory stocks were traded in but little on the open market. Even today, when these securities are traded in much more generally, there is a large number of companies whose stocks are very closely held and it requires some unusual occurrence to loosen them for trading on the open market.

A notable example of this is the Ford Motor Company. The Ford car is widely distributed, yet the two million dollar capital stock is almost entirely held by seven men. Another case is the H. H. Franklin Manufacturing Company, of

Syracuse. This company has $1,800,000 outstanding capital stock which is held largely by Mr. H. H. Franklin.

Further, out of a total of 81 companies reported upon (including the two above mentioned) at least 16, or practically 20 per cent, fall into the "closely held" class. Among these companies are the following:

Apperson Brothers
Consolidated Car Co.
Dodge Brothers
Federal Motor Truck
Ford Motor Co.195
Ford Motor Co. of Canada
H. H. Franklin Manufacturing Co.
Gramm Motor Truck Co.
Haynes Auto Co.
Kissel Motor Car Co.
Mitchell Lewis Motor Co.
Mutual Motors Co.
Pierce-Arrow Motor Car Co.
Republic Motor Truck Co.
Stearns Co.
Winton Co.

Some Leading Examples of Prices and Terms and Promotion Plans Upon Which Securities Were Put Out.

Perhaps one of the most notable examples of plans for flotation of securities was the 8 per cent cumulative convertible preferred stock of the Pierce-Arrow Motor Car Company, offered by prominent brokers in 1916. This stock must be redeemed at 125 up to the amount of cash paid on common stock in excess of $5.00 a share in any year. The preferred is convertible into common stock, share for share, at the holder's option (preferred stock $10,000,000) earnings five times preferred dividends; the common shares are without par value (common 250,000 shares).

Among other issues by banking houses of New York and other cities may be mentioned in 1912, General Motors Company's 6 per cent first lien sinking fund gold notes dated 1910, due 1915, $200,000,000 (since paid off); 1913 Chalmers Motor Company of Michigan, 7 per cent cumulative preferred stock (no bonds) $1,500,000, redeemable at $115 a share, earnings over 9½ times preferred interest; company taken over by new company in

1916. January, 1916, Willys-Overland Company convertible 7 per cent cumulative preferred stock, redeemable at $110, interest 6½ times earnings; November, 1916, Chalmers Motor Corporation of New York, shares at no par value, at $35 a share (264,000 shares), book value $29 a share, earnings, $5.40 a share; National Motor Car & Vehicle Company common shares at no par value (80,000 shares), no bonds, no preferred stock. Offered at $42.50 a share, earnings old company equal to 12½ per cent on new stock.

Most motor companies started with a small capitalization and business, and to provide additional working capital, as their business expanded, issued preferred or common stock.

Most of the better grade issues were for preferred stock, usually carrying with it a proviso that it could be retired at will at a stated price, some as high as $125.

Very few companies in the motor field have any bonded debt. Some companies which incurred such indebtedness in the past have paid it off; for example, the General Motors Company, and the Pierce-Arrow Motor Car Company.

The issues of securities by established motor companies have, as a rule, shown large liquid assets, and earning capacity record, and have been of the same general class.

In the automobile accessory line many flotations were put out in 1916 and a few in 1917, among which were:

(a) Edmunds & Jones Corporation.
(b) Perlman Rim Corporation.
(c) Motor Products Corporation.
(d) Fischer Body Corporation.
(e) United Alloy Steel Corporation.
(f) Transue & Williams Steel Forging Co.

(a) Edmunds & Jones Corporation (manufacturers of automobile lamps). This corporation issued $1,000,000 worth of preferred 7 per cent cumulative stock (no bonds), redeemable at $120, earning over six times preferred dividends.

(b) A somewhat unusual plan was the Perlman Rim Corporation (manufacturers of demountable automobile rims) which issued 100,000 shares of stock of no par value, divided into two classes as follows:

Class "A," having voting power.... 3,000 shares Common, no par value or voting power 97,000 shares

The estimated earnings of this company for 1917 are $3,000,000. In addition the company has been allowed claims for infringements sustained by the courts, amounting to $2,000,000.

(c) The Motor Products Corporation issued 100,000 shares, divided as follows:

Class "A," no par value, non voting . . 95,000 shares
Class "B," no par value, voting . . . . 5,000 shares

This corporation has taken over five companies manufacturing miscellaneous products, such as automobile radiators, windshields, etc. Their earnings for 1916 were $788,000.

(d) A more usual form is the $5,000,000 issue of 7 per cent cumulative preferred stock and 200,000 shares common stock, of the Fischer Body Corporation. It is not contemplated to pay a dividend on the common until the company has $1,000,000 surplus earnings. Its net profits for the year 1916 were $1,000,000 on a total volume of business amounting to $20,000,000. The preferred stock is redeemable at $120.

(e) The United Alloy Steel Corporation issued 525,000 shares without par value, of which 500,000 were used to acquire United Steel Company, manufacturing alloy steel parts for the automobile trade.

For expansion purposes to provide more adequate equipment to supply the increasing demand for its product, $4,000,000 additional cash capital was to be provided. The estimated net earnings for 1916 were about $7 a share on 500,000 shares.

(f) Transue & Williams Steel Forging Company issued 110,000 shares without par value. One hundred thousand shares and $750,000 cash was to be paid for company subscriptions at $45.50 a share. The net earnings for 7 months of 1916 were $648,026 or $12 a share.

Security Issues of Tire Companies.

Among the tire company stock issues a few leading examples may be cited.

The Firestone Tire & Rubber Company issued $5,000,000 of 6 per cent cumulative preferred stock. A sinking fund is provided to redeem this stock at $110, beginning 1921. There are no bonds, and the company is required to maintain at all times total net assets equal to 250 per cent and net quick assets equal to 150 per cent of the aggregate par value of this stock outstanding.

The earnings for 1916 were $4,482,554.52, or over seven times the dividend requirements on the total issue of preferred stock. This stock was sold at $107.

Another representative issue was that of the Fisk Rubber Company, which consisted of $5,000,000 of cumulative 7 per cent first preferred convertible stock. This is redeemable at $110 upon 60 days' notice.

The earnings for the year ending August 31, 1916, were $1,992,043, or three times the dividend requirements. There are no bonds or other form of funded debt.

One of the few instances of an issue of bonds by a tire company is the issue of $60,000,000 of 5 per cent gold bonds by the United States Rubber Company. Of course, tires are only a part of this company's output. The proceeds of the sale of these bonds are to be used to retire certain obligations of subsidiaries, to provide additional working capital, etc.

Newer Entrants Into the Security Market.

While in the foregoing chapter are noted some of the securities of representative manufacturers attracting the most pronounced attention, there are several others on the border line, or that have not as yet "arrived," and possibly may never do so.

There has, therefore, been so little activity in these securities, that examples of their flotations are negligible in this report.

Those most in the public eye are perhaps:

The Harroun Motors Corporation
The Emerson Motors Company, Inc.
The Ford Tractor Company, Inc., etc. etc.

Some Leading Examples of Appreciation or Depreciation in Value of Such Stocks Since They Were Put Out.

An example of depreciation in automobile stocks of an exaggerated type was that of the United States Motor Company, a combination of the Maxwell-Briscoe, Columbia, Stoddard-Dayton, Brush, and Sampson Companies. With an issue of about $35,000,000 stock, New York Curb prices in 1912 for the common ranged from 9 down to $1/16$ and for the preferred from $30½$ down to $¾$.

The properties of this company have since been taken over by the Maxwell Motors Companys, which issued the following securities:

$13,000,000 1st preferred

11,000,000 2nd preferred

13,000,000 common

The prices of these stocks have ranged as follows:

	1914	**1917**
Common	3	47½
1st preferred	22	64
2nd preferred	7	32

This instance gives an extreme example of the fluctuations possible in motor stocks in one year, in 1912 the market values reaching as high as 7,200 per cent of the value indicated at low. The re-organized company in less than five years showed a market value of possibly 38,000 per cent of the market value of the old company at its low, and 500 per cent of its value at its high.

These great increases in volume and values are what have made so many motor millionaires, and, conversely, have swept away some large fortunes.

Another instance is the stock of the Studebaker Corporation, which sold as low as 20 in 1914 and which now brings 102. Also the Kelly-Springfield Tire Company's stock rose from 50 to 299, due to their great increase in business and consequent large earnings.

General Comparison.

The attached chart, showing the average high and low prices of representative groups of securities during 1916, may be used

AS A COMPARISON OF THE AVERAGE SELLING PRICE OF THE MOTOR GROUP WITH THAT OF RAILROADS, INDUSTRIALS, AND MINING.

IT WILL BE SEEN THAT THE GREATEST FLUCTUATIONS OCCUR IN THE MINING, STEEL AND IRON STOCKS OF THE STANDARD LIST, AND THAT A SIMILAR FLUCTUATION OCCURS IN THE TIRE AND AUTOMOBILE STOCKS OF THE MOTOR GROUP.

THIS COMPARISON WOULD TEND TO SHOW THAT THE TIRE AND MOTOR STOCKS ARE STILL IN THE CLASS WHICH FLUCTUATES CONSIDERABLY AND THEREFORE, EXCEPT IN SPECIAL CASES, ARE MORE OR LESS SPECULATIVE. IN THIS LIGHT THESE FIGURES AND COMPARISONS ARE VERY INTERESTING AND MAY BE CAREFULLY CONSIDERED FROM THE INVESTMENT STANDPOINT.

THE FOLLOWING CHART COMPARES THE AVERAGE HIGH AND LOW PRICES OF REPRESENTATIVE GROUPS OF STOCKS DURING 1916 WITH SIMILAR GROUPS IN THE AUTOMOBILE FIELD:

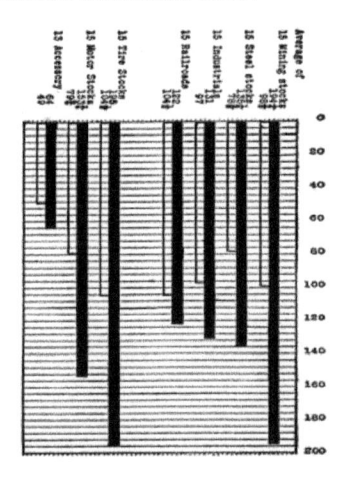

PRESENT TREND OF VALUES.

AFTER THE GREAT RISE IN PRICES, THE TREND OF VALUES OF THE SECURITIES OF MOTOR ACCESSORY AND TIRE COMPANIES, DURING THE FIRST QUARTER OF 1917, WAS GENERALLY DOWNWARD. DURING THE PAST TWO YEARS A LARGE NUMBER OF SUCH STOCKS HAVE BEEN PUT ON THE MARKET (SEE TABLE 1 AND 3) AND A GREAT DEAL OF SPECULATION HAS TAKEN PLACE, WITH THE RESULT THAT THE MARKET SEEMS OVERLOADED AT THE HIGH PRICES AT WHICH THE PUBLIC HAS BOUGHT THESE STOCKS. AT THE TIME OF THE MARKET REACTION AT THE END OF 1916, UNDER VARIOUS INFLUENCES, MOTOR STOCKS SUFFERED CONSIDERABLE LOSSES.

A few prominent instances may be cited. Studebaker, which sold as high as 67 in 1916, sold down to 102. Chevrolet Motor, whose high mark in 1916 was 278, sold down to 120. United Motors, which sold at 95 in 1916, sold down to 42¾. Similar conditions obtain through most of the list.

Among tire companies a few instances will show the same general downward tendency.

Lee Tire & Rubber Company's stock, which sold for 50¼ in 1915, is now selling around 23. Goodrich stock, which brought around 80 in 1915 and 1916, ranges between 51 and 58. The Kelly-Springfield Tire Company, which sold as high as 85¼ in 1916, now sells around 60.

During the year 1916, the range of high and of low of 25 leading railroad stocks traded in on the New York Exchange was between 76 and 85. Twenty-five leading industrials for the same period ranged between 90 and 113. The range of all the motor stocks traded in during this time was from 119 to 231; while that of the tire companies was from 45 to 76.

On the Curb, motor stocks in 1916 ranged from 39¾ to 57¾; tire stocks from 67 to 79; and accessories from 58 to 73, all of these figures representing average high and low of each class.

Possible Future Trend in Automobile Industry as a Basis for the Future Outlook for 1917 on its Securities.

As was stated in the opening introduction, economic conditions are perhaps the greatest factor to be considered in constructing any forecast for the operation of such an industry as that of the motor, motor accessory and tire group.

These economic conditions have mainly to do with:

(a) The increase of population, its effect reflected in increased registration, and automobile production.

(b) The uneven distribution of automobiles in the United States.

(a) Following is a chart which shows graphically the comparison between the growth of population, increased registration, and increased automobile production since 1911.

THE FOLLOWING CHART SHOWS THE RATE OF GROWTH OF AUTOMOBILE PRODUCTION AND REGISTRATION COMPARED WITH INCREASE IN POPULATION:

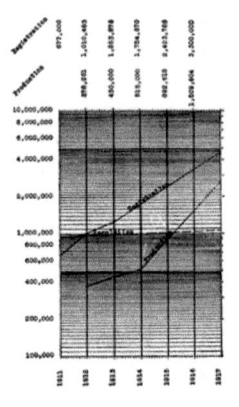

THIS WOULD INDICATE THAT, WHILE THE POPULATION IS GAINING SLOWLY AND CONSISTENTLY, THE PRODUCTION OF AUTOMOBILES HAS TAKEN A DECIDED JUMP, AND A NATURAL INFERENCE IS THAT, EVEN WITH SO REMARKABLE AN INDUSTRY AS THE MOTOR GROUP, IT IS BEGINNING TO PROVE FOOD FOR SPECULATION AS TO WHETHER OR NOT MANUFACTURERS, AT THE PRESENT INCREASING RATIO OF PRODUCTION AND DISTRIBUTION, WILL BRING A MORE OR LESS COMPLETE SATURATION OF THE PUBLIC, ABLE TO BUY AND SUPPORT PLEASURE AUTOMOBILES.

MANY CONSERVATIVE JUDGES HAVE FIGURED THAT THIS MAY NOT COME FOR SOME YEARS, POSSIBLE FIVE OR MORE. IT MAY BE THAT NEW CONDITIONS WILL ARISE TO PUT THAT PERIOD FURTHER AHEAD, OR INDEFINITELY POSTPONE IT.

(B) IN THIS CONNECTION, THE FOLLOWING CHART IS OF INTEREST. THIS SHOWS THE RATIO OF VOTING MEN TO EACH REGISTERED AUTOMOBILE IN THE UNITED STATES BY STATES.

THE FOLLOWING CHART SHOWS THE RATIO BY STATES OF MEN OVER 21 TO EACH REGISTERED AUTOMOBILE:

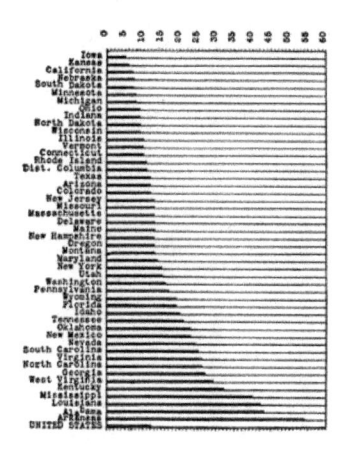

ATTENTION IS INVITED TO THE DIVERGING RANGE OF DISTRIBUTION. TERRITORIAL AND COMMUNITY ECONOMICS ACCOUNT FOR THIS VERY LARGELY. FOR EXAMPLE, AN ANALYSIS OF THREE SECTIONS WILL SHOW A DECIDED VARIATION, SAY FOR NEW YORK (WITH ONE AUTOMOBILE FOR 15 VOTING MEN); ARKANSAS (WITH ONE AUTOMOBILE FOR EVERY 54 VOTERS); AND ALABAMA (WITH ONE AUTOMOBILE FOR EVERY 43 VOTERS).

THE STATE OF NEW YORK IS VERY LARGELY INDUSTRIAL, AND ONE MIGHT COMMONLY INFER THAT, DUE TO THE GREAT WEALTH REPRESENTED IN THIS STATE, THE RATIO SHOULD BE MUCH SMALLER. STATES LIKE ARKANSAS, KANSAS AND IOWA ARE DISTINCTIVELY RURAL SECTIONS—WHERE THE POPULATION IS NOT SO CLUSTERED AS IN CITIES LIKE NEW YORK, AND AUTOMOBILE TRANSPORTATION IS MORE UTILITARIAN THAN A LUXURY OR PASTIME. FOR THIS REASON IT IS ESTIMATED THAT PRACTICALLY EVERY VOTER, ALMOST, IN KANSAS AND IOWA IS A POSSIBLE PROSPECT IN FIGURING FUTURE CONSUMPTION.

STILL ANOTHER DIVERSION NOTABLY EXISTS IN THE RATIO SHOWN FOR THE SOUTHERN STATES, AND THIS IS READILY EXPLAINED BY REASON OF A PAUCITY OF BUYING POWER, SINCE THE MAJORITY POPULATION IS NEGRO.

TO INDICATE HOW THE VARIOUS TYPES OF AUTOMOBILES HAVE BEEN DISTRIBUTED IN THREE DIFFERENT STATES, THE FOLLOWING CHART IS INCLUDED IN THIS REPORT.

THE FOLLOWING CHART SHOWS THE DISTRIBUTION OF LEADING MOTOR CARS IN DIFFERENT STATES:

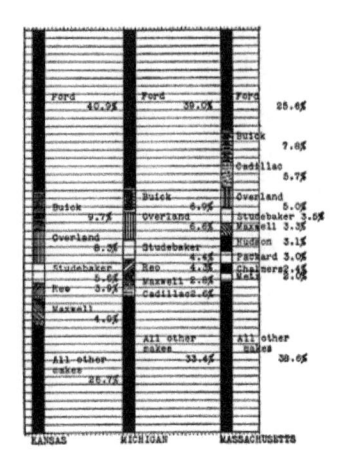

[Chart showing automobile market share by manufacturer in Kansas, Michigan, and Massachusetts]

THE FOLLOWING FACTORS MAY BE INSTRUMENTAL IN THE AUTOMOBILE INDUSTRY IN PREVENTING THE REACHING OF AN ABSOLUTE SATURATION POINT:

(1) INCREASE IN EARNING OR BUYING POWER OF THOSE NOW UNABLE TO SUPPORT AN AUTOMOBILE;

(2) A VERY LOW AVERAGE PRICE;

(3) PRODUCTION FINALLY BEING HELD AT THE POINT WHERE IT KEEPS PACE WITH THE INCREASE IN POPULATION;

(4) INCREASE IN THE UTILITARIAN NEED OF THE AUTOMOBILE.

IN MAKING UP A QUOTA FOR THE POSSIBLE CONSUMPTION IN THE AUTOMOBILE INDUSTRY, THE FOLLOWING CHART MAY BE CONSIDERED AS A CONSERVATIVE BASIS TO WORK ON.

THE FOLLOWING CHART SHOWS THE ESTIMATED AUTOMOBILE MARKET FOR 1917:

[Chart showing estimated automobile market for 1917, with columns: Number Buying Cars, Amount of Income, and Total Number of Persons]

Number Buying Cars	Amount of Income	Total Number of Persons
330,000	$600-999	3,360,000
1,250,000	$1000-1999	5,000,000
500,000	$2000-2999	1,500,000
270,000	$3000-4999	900,000
147,000	$5000-9999	420,000
60,000	$10,000 up	150,000
2,557,000		11,330,000

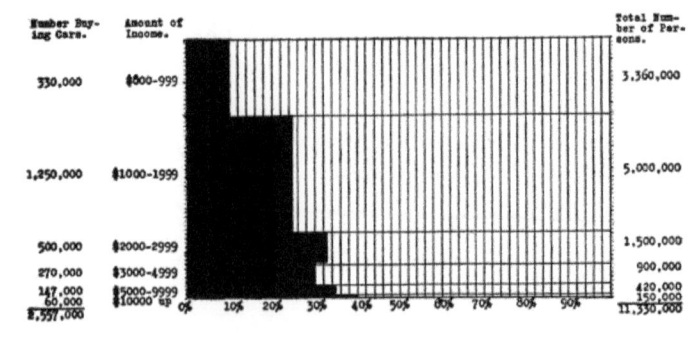

THERE BEING, THEREFORE SO MANY ELEMENTS ENTERING INTO THE QUESTION OF INFLUENCE UPON THIS GROUP OF SECURITIES, IT IS rather venturesome to presume any prediction for their future, for fear such prediction may prove unfounded, as have many former guesses on their probable rise and fall.

The immediate outlook for 1917 is at present somewhat baffling, aside from the economic tendencies, charted in this chapter, but there may be a change for improvement at any time in the motor car industry, especially if our government should place large orders for cars and supplies in the event of war, or the foreign trade should take on large quantities for the remainder of the year.

It must be remembered that the supply of parts for cars is now, and will be more and more, an extensive business of the motor car industry.

One prominent New York newspaper which censors very carefully its advertising is very cautious in handling offerings on motor stocks.

It might be safe to assume that motor stocks in well managed companies making popular cars will be as secure an investment for reasonable earnings on products as other industrials for some years to come and possibly indefinitely.

The future of automobile accessories is possibly not subject to fluctuations in the same degree, nor as apt to reach the saturation point as might be the development in the automobile industry, for the reason that with the increase in the number of cars in use, the purchase of many accessories will be made by car owners, even though the manufacturers should not continue to buy an increasing, or even equal, volume.

It is natural to expect that the earnings on and the price of automobile accessory stocks should therefore remain firm, if conditions of trade or competition do not unduly affect them.

The future of the tire industry and stocks seems reasonably secure, as unless some satisfactory substitutes for rubber tires are discovered, apparently an increasing number of tires for replacements, if not new cars, should be demanded each year.

The present earnings of the tire companies are very large and should continue favorable. It must be remembered that the cost of material and labor are as important considerations to this class of manufacturers as to all industrials, and that their undue rise in cost might affect the industry more or less temporarily. But as they have come to be classed as necessities, the prices would naturally adjust themselves to the cost of manufacture.

With all popular cars sold far in excess of their capacity, barring the interference or lack of transportation, labor friction, or other unexpected or disturbing elements, it is safe to assume that 1917 should be a record year in the motor, motor accessory and tire industries, and that their earnings should be reflected in the intrinsic and probably the market values of their securities.

CHAPTER VII.

PASSENGER AUTOMOBILES MANUFACTURED IN THE UNITED STATES.

The following is, as near as possible, a complete list of the passenger automobiles manufactured in the United States, with the number of cylinders and the retail price of each. New cars are being put on the market so rapidly that it is difficult to keep track of them.

The prices quoted may not be exact in every case, as manufacturers are putting up prices quite generally as this volume goes to press. They are the prices at which the cars sold for a long time, and they are given without the intention to be exact to the dollar, but merely as relative figures of retail cost.

An automobile quoted at $1,195 may have undergone a price raise to $1,350, but the former price quotation fixes the car's retail price status as compared with a car that sells for $360 or $550.

One hundred manufacturers are said to have raised their prices, and forty made increases from $10 to $700 on each car, the average advance being $146. Freight conditions and the uncertainties of the international situation were advanced as reasons for the increase.

Practically all the American manufacturers of tires also raised prices a second time within a year, the range of the last increase being from 6½ to 12 per cent. Where price is not given, it was not available.

		Cylinders	Price	
"Abbott-Detroit"	Abbott Corporation, Cleveland, O.	6	$1,195 to	$1,820
"Allen"	Allen Motor Car Co., Fostoria, O.	4	850 to	1,195
"Alter"	Alter Motor Car Co., Grand Haven, Mich.	4-6	675 to	850

"American"	American Motors Corporation, New York, N. Y.	6	1,285 and	845
"Ams-Sterling"	Sterling Automobile Manufacturing Co., New York, N. Y.	4	825 to	845
"Anderson"	Anderson Motor Co., Rock Hill, S. C.	6	1,250 and	1,275
"Apperson"	Apperson Bros. Auto Co., Kokomo, Ind.	6-8	1,690 to	2,000
"Arbenz"	Arbenz Motor Car Co., Chillicothe, O.			
"Auburn"	Auburn Automobile Co., Auburn, Ind.	6	1,145 to	1,785
"Austin"	Austin Automobile Co., Grand Rapids, Mich.	6-12	3,400 to	5,250
"Beardsley"	Beardsley Electric Co., Los Angeles, Cal. (Electric)	....	1,285 to	3,000
"Bell"	Bell Motor Car Co., York, Pa.	4	875	
"Ben-Hur"	Ben Hur Motor Co., Cleveland, O.	6	1,875 to	2,750
"Biddle"	Biddle Motor Car Co., Philadelphia, Pa.	4	2,285 to	3,900
"Bimel"	Bimel Automobile Co., Sidney, O.	4	550 to	995
"Bour-Davis"	Bour-Davis Motor Car Co., Detroit, Mich.	6	1,250 to	1,500
"Brewster"	Brewster & Co., New York, N. Y.	4	6,500 to	7,900
"Briscoe"	Briscoe Motor Corporation, Jackson, Mich.	4-8	685 to	985
"Brunswick"	Brunswick Motor Car Co.,			

	New York, N. Y.			
"Buick"	Buick Motor Co., Flint, Mich.	4-6	660 to	1,835
"Bush"	Bush Motor Co., Chicago, Ill.	4	725	
"Cadillac"	Cadillac Motor Car Co., Detroit, Mich.	8	2,240 to	3,910
"Cameron"	Cameron Car Co., Norwalk, Conn.	6	1,250	
"Case"	J. I. Case Threshing Machine Co., Racine, Wis.	4	1,190	
"C-B"	Carter Brothers Co., Hyattsville, Md.	6-8	700 to	1,000
"Chalmers"	Chalmers Motor Car Co., Detroit, Mich.	6	1,090 to	2,550
"Chandler"	Chandler Motor Car Co., Cleveland, O.	6	1,395 to	2,695
"Chevrolet"	Chevrolet Motor Co., Flint, Mich.	4-8	490 to	1,285
"Classic"	Classic Motor Co., Chicago, Ill.			
"Coey Flyer"	Coey Motor Co., Chicago, Ill.	4	695	
"Cole 8"	Cole Motor Car Co., Indianapolis, Ind.	8	1,695 to	2,295
"Columbia"	Columbia Motor Co., Detroit, Mich.	6	on application	
"Crawford"	Crawford Automobile Co., Hagerstown, Md.	6	1,750 to	2,250
"Crockett"	The J. B. Co., New York City (exported only)			
"Crow Elkhart"	Crow Elkhart Motor Car Co., Elkhart, Ind.	4	795 and	845

"Crowther-Duryea"	Crowther Motors Corporation, Rochester, N. Y.	4	650	
"Cunningham"	James Cunningham Son & Co., Rochester, N. Y.	8	3,750 to	7,500
"Daniels"	Daniels Motor Car Co., Reading, Pa.	8	2,600 to	4,200
"Davis"	George W. Davis Motor Car Co., Richmond, Ind.	6	1,195 to	1,795
"Detroit"	Anderson Electric Car Co., Detroit, Mich. (Electric)	...	1,875 to	2,475
"Detroiter"	Detroiter Motor Car Co., Detroit, Mich.	6	1,195 to	1,495
"Dey"	Dey Electric Corporation, New York, N. Y. (Electric)			
"Dispatch"	Dispatch Motor Car Co., Minneapolis, Minn.	4	1,135 to	1,400
"Dixie"	Dixie Manufacturing Co., Vincennes, Ind.			
"Dixie Flyer"	Dixie Motor Car Co., Louisville, Ky.	4	840 to	1,275
"Doble"	General Engineering Co., Detroit, Mich. (Steam)	4-7	1,800	
"Dodge"	Dodge Bros., Detroit, Mich.	4	785 to	1,185
"Dorris"	Dorris Motor Car Co., St. Louis, Mo.	6	2,475	
"Dort"	Dort Motor Car Co., Flint, Mich.	4	695 to	1,065
"Downing"	Downing Motor Car Co., Detroit, Mich.			
"Drexel"	Drexel Motor Car Corporation, Chicago, Ill.	4	985 to	1,650
"Drummond"	Drummond Motor Co.,	8	1,600	

	Omaha, Neb.			
"Dunn"	Dunn Motor Works, Ogdensburg, N. Y.	4	295	
"Duryea Gem"	Duryea Motors, Inc., Philadelphia, Pa. (3 wheels)	2	250	
"Eagle Rotary"	Eagle-Macomber Motor Car Co., Sandusky, O.	5	700	
"Economy"	Economy Motor Co., Tiffin, O.	4-8	985 to	1,350
"Elcar"	Elkhart Carriage & Motor Car Co., Elkhart, Ind.	4	845	
"Elgin"	Elgin Motor Car Co., Chicago, Ill.	6	985	
"Emerson"	Emerson Motors Co., New York, N. Y.	4	470	
"Empire"	Empire Automobile Co., Indianapolis, Ind.	4-6	985 to	1,095
"Enger"	Enger Motor Car Co., Cincinnati, O.	12	1,295	
"Erie"	Erie Motor Car Co., Painesville, O.	4	795	
"Fageol"	Fageol Motors Co., Oakland, Cal. (Aviation motor)	6	9,500 to	12,500
"F. I. A. T."	Fiat, Poughkeepsie, N. Y.	5-7	4,850 to	6,300
"Ford"	Ford Motor Co., Detroit, Mich.	4	345 to	645
"Ford"	Ford Motor Co. of Canada, Ltd., Ford, Ont.	4	345 to	645
"Franklin"	Franklin Automobile Co., Syracuse, N. Y.	6	1,800 to	3,000
"Fritchie"	Fritchie Electric Co., Denver, Colo. (Electric)	....	2,400 to	3,200

"Frontenac"	Frontenac Motor Co., Detroit, Mich. (Racing)	4	8,000 to	10,000
"F. B. P."	Porter, Finley Robertson Co., Port Jefferson, N. Y.	4	6,000	
"Glide"	Bartholomew Company, Peoria, Ill.	6	1,195 to	1,395
"Grant"	Grant Motor Car Corporation, Cleveland, O.	6	875 to	1,100
"Hackett"	Hackett Motor Car Co., Jackson, Mich.	4	888	
"Hal Twelve"	Hal Motor Car Co., Cleveland, O.	12	2,600 to	5,000
"Halladay"	Barley Motor Car Co., Streator, Ill.	6	1,185 to	1,650
"Harroun"	Harroun Motors Corporation, Detroit, Mich.	4	595	
"Harvard"	Harvard Pioneer Motor Car Corporation, Troy, N. Y.	4	750	
"Hatfield"	Cortland Cart & Carriage Co., Sidney, N. Y.	4	875	
"Haynes"	Haynes Automobile Co., Kokomo, Ind.	6-12	1,485 to	2,750
"Hewitt"	Hewitt Motor Co., New York, N. Y.			
"Hollier"	Lewis Spring & Axle Co., Jackson, Mich.	6-8	895 to	1,185
"Homer-Laughlin"	Homer-Laughlin Engineers' Corporation, Los Angeles, Cal.	8	1,050	
"Howard"	The A. Howard Co., Galion, O.			
"Hudson"	Hudson Motor Car Co., Detroit, Mich.	6	1,650 to	3,025

"Hupmobile"	Hupp Motor Car Corporation, Detroit, Mich.	4	1,185 to	1,735
"Hupp-Yeats"	Hupp-Yeats Electric Car Co., Detroit, Mich. (Electric)	....	1,500 to	1,750
"Interstate"	Interstate Motor Co., Muncie, Ind.	4	850 to	1,250
"Jackson"	Jackson Automobile Co., Jackson, Mich.	8	1,295 to	1,395
"Jeffery"	Nash Motors Co., Kenosha, Wis.	4-6	1,095 to	1,630
"Jones"	Jones Motor Car Co., Wichita, Kas.	6	1,475	
"Jordan"	Jordan Motor Car Co., Cleveland, O.	6	1,650 to	3,000
"Kent"	Kent Motors Corporation, Newark, N. J.	4	985	
"King"	King Motor Car Co., Detroit, Mich.	8	1,350 to	1,900
"Kissel Kar"	Kissel Motor Car Co., Hartford, Wis.	6	1,195 to	2,100
"Kline Kar"	Kline Car Corporation, Richmond, Va.	6	1,175 to	1,195
"Lambert"	Buckeye Manufacturing Co., Anderson, Ind.	4-6	685 to	985
"Laurel"	Laurel Motor Car Co., Richmond, Ind.	4	850 to	895
"Lenox"	Lenox Motor Car Co., Boston, Mass.	6	on application	
"Leslie"	Leslie Motor Car Co., Detroit, Mich. (Kerosene)			
"Lexington"	Lexington-Howard Co., Connersville, Ind.	6	1,185 to	2,875
"Liberty"	Liberty Motor Car Co.,	6	1,095 to	2,350

	Detroit, Mich.			
"Locomobile"	Locomobile Co. of America, Bridgeport, Conn.	6	4,600 to	6,800
"Lozier"	Lozier Motor Co., Detroit, Mich.	4-6	1,695 to	4,650
"Luverne"	Luverne Automobile Co., Luverne, Minn.	6	1,500	
"Lyons-Knight"	Lyons-Atlas Co., Indianapolis, Ind.			
"Macon"	All Steel Motor Car Co., Macon, Mo.	4	875 to	975
"Madison"	Madison Motors Co., Anderson, Ind.	6	1,050 to	1,150
"Maibohm"	Maibohm Motors Co., Racine, Wis.	4	795	
"Majestic"	Majestic Motor Co., New York, N. Y.	....	on application	
"Marion Handley"	Mutual Motors Co., Jackson, Mich.	6	1,275 to	1,575
"Marmon"	Nordyke & Marmon Co., Indianapolis, Ind.	6	3,050 to	5,800
"Maxwell"	Maxwell Motor Co., Detroit, Mich.	4	620 to	985
"McFarlan"	McFarlan Motor Co., Connersville, Ind.	6	3,500 to	5,300
"Mercer"	Mercer Automobile Co., Trenton, N. J.	4	3,250 to	5,000
"Metz"	Metz Company, Waltham, Mass.	4	600	
"Milburn"	Milburn Wagon Co., Toledo, O. (Electric)	....	1,285 to	1,995
"Mitchell"	Mitchell Motors Co., Racine, Wis.	6	1,150 to	2,785

"Mohawk"	Mohawk Motor Corporation, New Orleans, La.	4-6	985 to	1,150
"Moline-Knight"	Moline Automobile Co., East Moline, Ill.	4	1,450 to	2,400
"Monarch"	Monarch Motor Car Co., Detroit, Mich.	8	1,500	
"Monitor"	Monitor Motor Car Co., Columbus, O.	4-6	895 to	1,095
"Monroe"	Monroe Motor Co., Pontiac, Mich.	4	565 and	985
"Moon"	Moon Motor Car Co., St. Louis, Mo.	6	1,295 to	2,350
"Moore"	Moore Motor Co., Minneapolis, Minn.	4	550	
"Morse"	Morse Cyclecar Co., Pittsburgh, Pa.	2	300 and	350
"Murray"	Murray Motor Car Co., Pittsburgh, Pa.	8	2,000 to	2,500
"Napoleon"	Napoleon Auto Manufacturing Co., Napoleon, Ohio	4	735 to	845
"National"	National Motor Car & Vehicle Corporation	6-12	1,750 to	2,800
"New Era"	New Era Engineering Co., Joliet, Ill.	4	685	
"Norwalk"	Norwalk Motor Car Co., Martinsburg, W. Va.			
"Ogren Six"	Ogren Motor Works, Inc., Chicago, Ill.	6	2,500	
"Oakland"	Oakland Motor Car Co., Pontiac, Mich.	6-8	875 to	1,585
"Ohio"	Ohio Electric Car Co., Toledo, O. (Electric)	....	2,400 to	3,250

"Oldsmobile"	Olds Motor Works, Lansing, Mich.	8	1,295 to	1,850
"Olympian"	Olympian Motors Co., Pontiac, Mich.	4	845	
"Overland"	Willys-Overland Co., Toledo, O.	4-6	665 to	1,585
"Owen Magnetic"	Baker B. & L. Co., Cleveland, O.	6	3,300 to	5,200
"Packard"	Packard Motor Car Co., Detroit, Mich.	12	3,050 to	5,150
"Paige"	Paige-Detroit Motor Car Co., Detroit, Mich.	6	1,175 to	2,750
"Partin-Palmer"	Commonwealth Motors Co., Chicago, Ill.	4	495 to	695
"Paterson"	W. A. Paterson Co., Flint, Mich.	6	1,095 to	1,125
"Path-finder"	Pathfinder Co., Indianapolis, Ind.	12	3,250	
"Peerless"	Peerless Motor Car Co., Cleveland, O.	8	1,890 to	3,260
"Pennsy"	Pennsy Motors Co., Pittsburgh, Pa.	4	855	
"Phianna"	Phianna Motors Co., Newark, N. J.	4	5,000 to	6,000
"Pierce-Arrow"	Pierce-Arrow Motor Car Co., Buffalo, N. Y.	6	4,600 to	7,600
"Pilliod"	Pilliod Motor Co., Toledo, O.	4	1,485	
"Pilot"	Pilot Motor Car Co., Richmond, Ind.	6	1,150	
"Premier"	Premier Motor Corporation, Indianapolis, Ind.	6	1,885 to	3,150
"Princess"	Princess Motor Car	4	775	

	Corporation, Detroit, Mich.			
"Pullman"	Pullman Motor Car Co., York, Pa.	4	825 to	1,150
"Rauch & Lang"	Baker R. & L. Co., Cleveland, O. (Electric)	....	2,800 to	3,000
"Regal"	Regal Motor Car Co., Detroit, Mich.	4	745	
"Reo"	Reo Motor Car Co., Lansing, Mich.	4-6	875 to	1,750
"Richard"	Richard Auto Manufacturing Co., Cleveland, O.	4	7,500	
"Richmond"	The Wayne Works, Richmond, Ind.	6	on application	
"Roamer"	Barley Motor Co., Streator, Ill.	6	1,850	
"Rose"	Rose Automobile Co., Detroit, Mich.	8	1,550	
"Saurer"	Saurer Motor Co., New York, N. Y.			
"Saxon"	Saxon Motor Corporation, Detroit, Mich.	4-6	495 to	1,250
"Scripps-Booth"	Scripps Booth Corporation, Detroit, Mich.	4-8	825 to	2,575
"Seneca"	Seneca Motor Car Co., Fostoria, O.	4	735	
"Simplicity"	Evansville Automobile Co., Evansville, Ind.			
"Simplex"	Simplex Automobile Co., New York, N. Y. (Chassis only)	6	6,000	
"Singer"	Singer Motor Car Co., New York, N. Y.	6	3,800 to	5,300
"Standard"	Standard Steel Car Co.,	8	1,950 to	2,000

	Pittsburgh, Pa.			
"Stanley Steam Car"	Stanley Motor Carriage Co., Newton, Mass. (Steam)	....	2,200 to	2,300
"States"	States Motor Car Manufacturing Co., Kalamazoo, Mich.	4	845	
"Stearns"	F. B. Stearns Co., Cleveland, O.	4-8	1,450 to	3,500
"Stephens"	Stephens Motor Branch, Moline Plow Co., Freeport, Ill.	6	1,150	
"Studebaker"	Studebaker Corporation, Detroit, Mich.	4-6	930 to	2,600
"Stutz"	Stutz Motor Car Co., Indianapolis, Ind.	4	2,275 to	2,550
"Sun"	Sun Motor Car Co., Elkhart, Ind.	6	1,095 to	1,295
"Thomas"	E. R. Thomas Motor Car Co., Buffalo, N. Y.	6	4,000 to	5,000
"Velie"	Velie Motors Corporation, Moline, Ill.	6	1,115 to	2,200
"Waco"	Western Automobile Co., Seattle, Wash.	4	950	
"Westcott"	Westcott Motor Car Co., Springfield, O.	6	1,500 to	2,190
"White"	White Motor Co., Cleveland, O.	4	4,600 up	
"Willys-Knight"	Willys-Overland Co., Toledo, O.	6	1,325	
"Willys-Knight"	Willys-Overland Co., Toledo, O.	4-8	1,285 to	1,950
"Winton"	Winton Co., Cleveland, O.	6	2,685 to	4,750
"Woods"	Woods Mobilette Co.,	4	380	

	Chicago, Ill.		
"Wood's Dual Power"	Woods Motor Vehicle Co., Chicago, Ill. (Electric)	....	2,650
"Yale Eight"	Saginaw Motor Car Co., Saginaw, Mich.	8	1,550

CHAPTER VIII.

GASOLINE TRUCKS AND DELIVERY CARS MANUFACTURED IN THE UNITED STATES.

THIS CHAPTER IS REPRINTED FROM *EVERYBODY'S MAGAZINE* THROUGH THE COURTESY OF ITS PUBLISHERS, WHO WERE KIND ENOUGH TO GRANT THIS PERMISSION. THIS LIST WAS COMPILED SO ABLY BY THE EDITORIAL STAFF OF *EVERYBODY'S MAGAZINE* THAT IT COULD NOT POSSIBLY HAVE BEEN IMPROVED UPON FOR PUBLICATION IN THIS VOLUME.

A PART OF THE INFORMATION IN THE PRECEDING CHAPTER IS ALSO FROM *EVERYBODY'S MAGAZINE*, AND IS REPRINTED HERE THROUGH THE COURTESY OF THE PUBLISHERS.

THE CARS AND TRUCKS LISTED HAVE FOUR CYLINDERS, UNLESS STATED OTHERWISE. THE PRICES ARE THOSE THAT WERE IN EFFECT PRIOR TO APRIL 1, 1917.

	Capacity Tons	Prices
"Acason," Acason Motor Truck Co., Detroit, Mich., 2 models. Chassis only. Hotchkiss drive	2 and 3½	On application
"Acme," Cadillac Auto Truck Co., Cadillac, Mich., 3 models. Bodies extra. Worm drive	1 to 3½	$1575 and $3000
"Armleder," The O. Armleder Co., Cincinnati, Ohio, 2 models. Bodies extra. Worm drive	2 and 3½	2800 and 3500
"Atlas," Martin Carriage Works, York, Pa., 1 model. Bodies extra. Hotchkiss drive	1000 to 1500 lbs.	750
"Atterbury," Atterbury Motor Car Co., Buffalo, N. Y., 4 models. Chassis 232only. Worm drive	1 to 3½	1875 to 3375
"Autocar," The Autocar Co.,	1½ to 2	$1650

Ardmore, Pa., 1 model, 2 cylinders. Bodies extra. Shaft drive			
"Available," Available Truck Co., Chicago, Ill., 4 models. Worm drive	1 to 5	1700 to	$4400
"Avery," Avery Company, Peoria, Ill., 3 models. Bodies extra. Chain drive	2 to 5	2700 to	4500
"Beck," Beck & Sons, Cedar Rapids, Iowa, 4 models. Bodies extra. Internal Gear drive	1 to 2½	1080 to	2000
"Beech Creek," Beech Creek Truck & Auto Co., Beech Creek, Pa., 1 model. Chassis only. Gear drive	3	3850	
"Bessemer," Bessemer Motor Truck Co., Grove City, Pa., 4 models. Bodies extra. Worm drive	1 to 5	1075 to	4000
"Brinton," Brinton Motor Truck Co., Philadelphia, Pa., 2 models. Chassis, including Cab	1 and 2½	995 to	2250
"Briscoe," Briscoe Motor Corp., Jackson, Mich., 2 models. Complete Shaft drive	¾	700 and	725
"Brockway," Brockway Motor Truck Co., Cortland, N. Y., 6 models. Complete. Worm drive	1 to 2½	1500 to	2250
"Burford," Burford Motor Truck Co., Fremont, Ohio, 2 models. Chassis only. Worm and Internal Gear drive	2 and 4	2250 to	3600
"Chase," Chase Motor Truck Co., Syracuse, N. Y., 5 models. Complete. Worm drive	¾ to 3½	1500 to	3200

"Coey," Coey Motor Co., Chicago, Ill., 1 model. Express bodies extra. Shaft drive	½	695		
"Collier," Collier Motor Truck Co., Sandusky, Ohio, 1 model. With or without body. Direct bevel drive	¾	900	and	995
"Commerce," Commerce Motor Car Co., Detroit, Mich., 2 models, 6 bodies. Internal and Bevel Gear drive	¾ and 1	875	to	1140
"Corbitt," Corbitt Motor Truck Co., Henderson, N. C., 6 models. Bodies extra. Worm drive	1 to 5	1450	to	3850
"Couple Gear," Couple Gear Freight Wheel Co., Grand Rapids, Mich., 3 models. Four-wheel drive. Complete. (Gas electric.)	3½ to 7	5200	to	6000
"Crane & Breed," Crane & Breed Mfg. Co., Cincinnati, Ohio, Funeral cars. etc. 6 cylinders		3000	to	4200
"Crowther-Duryea," Crowther Motor Co., Rochester, N. Y., 1 model. Complete. Roller drive	½	600		
"Dart," Dart Motor Truck Co., Waterloo, Iowa, 3 models. Bodies extra. Worm drive	½ to 2½	1200	to	2470
"Dayton," Dayton Motor Truck Co., Dayton, Ohio, 6 models. Chain and Worm drive	2 to 7½	2650	to	4950
"D-E," Day-Elder Motors Co., Newark, N. J., 3 models. Bodies extra. Worm drive	½ to 1½	975	to	1800

"De Kalb," DeKalb Wagon Co., DeKalb, Ill., 2 models. Bodies extra	2 to 2½	2100	to	2450
"Denby," Denby Motor Truck Co., Detroit, Mich., 4 models. 1-ton complete. Other bodies extra. Internal gear drive	1 to 2½	1275	to	2150
"Den Mo," The Denneen Motor Co., Cleveland, Ohio., 1 model. Chassis only. Internal gear drive	1¼ to 1⅞	1385		
"Diamond T," Diamond T Motor Car Co., Chicago, Ill., 5 models. Chassis only	1 to 5	1485	to	4100
"Dispatch," Dispatch Motor Car Co., Minneapolis, Minn., 2 models. Complete. Internal chain drive	¾	1100	to	1200
"Dorris," Dorris Motor Car Co., St. Louis, Mo., 1 model. Chassis only. Worm drive	2	2185		
"Downing," Downing Motor Truck Co., Detroit, Mich., 2 models	¾ to 1½	600	and	750
"Duplex 4-Wheel Drive," Duplex Truck Co., Lansing, Mich., 1 model.	3½	3600		
"Ellsworth," Mills-Ellsworth Co., Keokuk, Iowa, 1 model. Complete	½	695	and	720
"Erie," Erie Motor Truck Mfg. Co., Erie, Pa., 3 models. Bodies extra. Worm drive	1 to 3½	1500	to	3000
"Fargo," Fargo Motor Car Co., Chicago, Ill., 1 model. Bodies extra. Internal Gear drive	2	1390		
"F. W. D.," Four-Wheel Drive	3	4000		

Auto Co., Clintonville, Wis., 1 model. Chassis only. Bevel Gear drive			
"Federal," Federal Motor Truck Co., Detroit, Mich., 5 models. Bodies extra. Worm drive	1 to 5	1650 to	4000
"Gabriel," Gabriel Auto Co., Cleveland, Ohio, 3 models. Chassis only. Worm drive	¾ to 1½	1600 to	2300
"Garford," The Garford Motor Truck Co., Lima, Ohio, 10 models. Bodies extra. Worm and Chain drive	1 to 10	1750 to	6000
"Gary," The Gary Motor Truck Co., Gary, Ind., 5 models. Worm drive	¾ to 3½	On application	
"Globe," Globe Motor Truck Co., Northville Mich., 2 models, 6 cylinders. Chassis only. Worm and Internal Gear drive	1 and 2	1375 and	1985
"G. M. C.," General Motors Truck Co., Pontiac, Mich., 6 models. Bodies extra. Chain and Worm drive	¾ to 5	1150 to	4150
"Gramm-Bernstein," Gramm-Bernstein Motor Truck Co., Lima, Ohio., 6 models. Bodies extra. Worm drive	1 to 6	On application	
"Hahn," Hahn Motor Truck & Wagon Co., Hamburg, Pa., 4 models. Worm drive	¾ to 3½	1150 to	4150
"Hall," Lewis Hall Iron Works, Detroit, Mich., 3 models. Worm and Chain drive	2 to 5	2000 to	3600
"Harley-Davidson," Harley-Davidson Motor Co., Milwaukee, Wis., 3 models.	300 lbs.	310 to	380

Cycle delivery

"Harvey," Harvey Motor Truck Company, Harvey, Ill., 3 models. Bodies extra. Worm drive	2½ to 5	2500	to	4000
"Hatfield," Cortland Cart & Carriage Co., Sidney, N. Y., 3 models. Complete. Bevel Gear drive	1000 lbs.	765	to	820
"Hawkeye," Hawkeye Mfg. Co., Sioux City, Iowa, 1 model. Chassis only. Internal Gear drive	1¼	1300		
"Henderson Bros." Henderson Bros., North Cambridge, Mass., 2 models. Chassis only. Worm drive	1200 lbs. and 1 ton	1225	and	1500
"Hewitt-Ludlow," Hewitt-Ludlow Auto Co., San Francisco, Cal. 5 models. Chassis only. Worm and Chain drive. Also tractors	1 to 5	1800	to	4550
"Hoover," Hoover Wagon Co., York, Pa., 1 model. Bodies to order. Worm drive	¾	1190		
"Horner," Detroit-Wyandotte Motor Truck Co., Wyandotte, Mich., 4 models. Bodies extra. Worm drive	1 to 5	2350	to	4200
"Houghton," The Houghton Motor Car Co., Marion, Ohio, hearses and ambulances. Worm drive	¾	1585	to	1650
"Hurlburt," Hurlburt Motor Co., New York City, N. Y., 5 models. Worm drive. Chassis only	1½ to 7	2250	to	5000
"Independent," Independent Motors Co., Port Huron, Mich.,	1 and 2	1385	and	1850

2 models. Worm drive

"Indiana," Indiana Truck Co., Marion, Ind., 4 models. Bodies extra	1 to 5	1385 to	3500
"International," International Harvester Co., Chicago, Ill., 2 models. Bodies extra. Internal Gear drive.	¾ and 1	1225 and	1500
"Jeffery," The Nash Motors Co., Kenosha, Wis., 3 models. Bodies extra. Bevel and Internal Gear drive	¾ to 2	965 to	2850
"Kearns," Kearns Motor Truck Co., Beavertown, Pa., 1 model. Complete. Shaft drive	1000 lbs.	785	
"Kelly," The Kelly-Springfield Motor Truck Co., Springfield, Ohio, 8 models. Chassis only. Worm and Chain drive	1½ to 6	2250 to	4600
"King," A. R. King Mfg. Co., Kingston, N. Y., 1 model. Chassis only. Chain drive	3½	2600	
"Kissel," The Kissel Motor Co., Hartford, Wis., 7 models. Bodies extra. Worm and bevel drive	¾ to 5	950 to	2850
"Kleiber," Kleiber & Co., Inc., San Francisco, Cal., 5 models. Bodies extra. Worm drive	1½ to 5	2250 to	4500
"Knickerbocker," Knickerbocker Motors, Inc., N. Y. City, 3 models. Bodies extra. Worm drive. Also 3-ton tractor	3 to 5	3500 to	4500
"Koehler," H. J. Koehler Motors Corp., Newark, N. J., 1 model. Bodies extra. Internal Gear drive	1	895	
"Koenig & Luhrs," Koenig &	¾	900	

Luhrs Wagon Co., Quincy, Ill., 1 model

"Krebs," Krebs Commercial Car Co., Clyde, Ohio, 4 models. Bodies extra. Worm drive	1½ to 5	2050	to	4000
"Lambert," Buckeye Mfg. Co., Anderson, Ind., 5 models. Also tractors. Chain drive	½ to 2	900	to	2200
"Lamson," Zeitler & Lamson Truck Co., Chicago, Ill., 4 models. Chassis only. Worm drive. Also tractor and dumping equipment	1 to 5	1550	to	4350
"Lange," Lange Motor Truck Co., Pittsburgh, Pa., 2 models. Bodies extra	1 to 3½	1850	to	2450
"Larrabee," Larrabee-Deyo Motor Truck Co., Binghamton, N. Y., 4 models. Bodies extra. Worm drive	1 to 2½	1600	to	3300
"Lenox," Lenox Motor Car Co., Boston, Mass., 2 models, 4 and 6 cylinders. 12 to 28 tons haulage	Tractor	On application		
"Leslie," Leslie Motor Car Co., Detroit, Mich., 1 model. Kerosene fuel	¾	On application		
"Lippard-Stewart," Lippard-Stewart Motor Car Co., Buffalo, N. Y., 5 models. Bodies extra. Worm drive	½ to 2	1000	to	2600
"Little Giant," Chicago Pneumatic Tool Co., Chicago, Ill., 3 models. Bodies extra. Chain and Worm drive	1 to 5	1400	to	4250
"Maccar," Maccar Truck Co., Scranton, Pa., 4 models. Chassis	1 to 5½	2100	to	4150

only. Worm drive

"Mack," International Motor Co., N. Y. City, 6 models. Chassis only. Chain and Worm drive	1 to 7½	2150	to	4600
"Maxim," Maxim Motor Co., Middleboro, Mass., 2 models, 4 and 6 cylinders. Bodies extra. Fire apparatus special. Worm drive	2	2500	and	3500
"M. H. C.," Michigan Hearse & Motor Co., Grand Rapids, Mich., funeral cars, etc., 6 cylinders		On application		
"The Menominee," Menominee Motor Truck Co., Menominee, Mich., 5 models. Bodies extra. Worm drive.	¾ to 3½	1295	to	2775
"Mercury," The Mercury Mfg. Co., Chicago, Ill., tractor, 3 models		3400		
"Modern," Bowling Green Motor Truck Co., Bowling Green, Ohio, 2 models. Chassis only. Worm drive	1 and 2	1500	and	2000
"Moeller," New Haven Truck & Auto Works, New Haven, Conn., 3 models. Bodies extra. Chain drive	1½ to 5	2500	to	4500
"Mogul," Mogul Motor Truck Co., St. Louis, Mo., 4 models. Bodies extra. Worm and Chain drive	1½ to 6	1600	to	4000
"Monarch," Monarch Light Truck Co., Milwaukee, Wis., 2 models. Bodies extra. Worm drive	½ and 1	750	and	950

"Moon," Jos. W. Moon Buggy Co., St. Louis, Mo., 2 models. Bodies extra. Chain and Shaft drive	¾ to 1½	950 and	1650
"Moreland," Moreland Motor Truck Co., Los Angeles, Cal., 4 models. Chassis only. Worm drive	¾ to 5	1290 to	4250
"Morton," Morton Truck and Tractor Co., Harrisburg, Pa., 1 model. Chassis only. Worm drive	3	4250	
"Nelson Lemoon," Nelson & LeMoon, Chicago, Ill., 4 models. Worm drive. Chassis only	1 to 5	1700 to	4200
"Netco," New England Truck Co., Fitchburg, Mass., 3 models, 4 and 6 cylinders. Bodies and fire apparatus extra. Worm	drive 1½ to 2	2350 to	4250
"Niles," Niles Car & Mfg. Co., Niles, Ohio, 2 models. Bodies to order. Worm drive	1 and 2	1500 to	2400
"Northwestern," Star Carriage Co., Seattle, Wash., 1 model. Bodies extra. Worm drive	1½	2150	
"Old Hickory," Kentucky Wagon Mfg. Co., Louisville, Ky., 1 model. Bodies extra. Bevel Gear drive	1250 lbs.	825	
"Old Reliable," Old Reliable Motor Truck Co., Chicago, Ill., 12 models. Bodies and trailers extra. Chain and Worm drive	1½ to 7	1950 to	5000
"Packard," Packard Motor Car Co., Detroit, Mich., 7 models. Bodies extra. Worm drive	1 to 6	2200 to	4550
"Palmer-Moore," Palmer-Moore Co., Syracuse, N. Y., 2 models.	1 and 2	1075 and	1675

Bodies extra. Internal Gear drive

"Paragan," Paragan Motor Truck Co., Auburn, Ind., 1 model, 4 bodies	1	975	
"Peerless," Peerless Motor Car Co., Cleveland, Ohio, 6 models. Bodies and tractors extra. Chain and Worm drive	2 to 6	3000 to	5000
"Pierce-Arrow," Pierce-Arrow Motor Car Co., Buffalo, N. Y., 2 models. Bodies extra. Worm drive		2 and 5	3000 to 4500
"Piggins," Piggins Motor Truck Co., Racine, Wis., 4 models. Chassis only. Enclosed Spur Gear drive	1 to 5	1750 to	3850
"Rainer," Rainer Motor Corp., N. Y. City, 1 model. Bodies extra. Worm drive	½	875	
"Reo," Reo Motor Car Co., Lansing, Mich., 2 models ¾-ton with express body. Other, chassis only. Shaft and Chain drive	¾ and 5	1000 and	1650
"Republic," Republic Motor Truck Co., Alma, Mich., 4 models, ¾-ton complete. Other bodies extra. Internal Gear drive	¾ to 5	750 to	2550
"Riker," The Locomobile Co. of America, Bridgeport, Conn., 2 models. Bodies, tractor, etc., extra. Worm drive	3 and 4	3600 to	3750
"Rowe," Rowe Motor Mfg. Co., Downington, Pa., 5 models. Chassis only. Fire apparatus special	1 to 5	2450 to	4500

"Rush," Rush Motor Truck Co., Philadelphia, Pa., 1 model. Bodies extra. Bevel Gear drive.	½		735	
"Sandow," Sandow Motor Truck Co., Chicago, Ill., 4 models. Bodies extra. Worm drive	1 to 3½	1150	to	3250
"Sanford," Sanford Motor Truck Co., Syracuse, N. Y., 3 models. Chassis only. Internal Gear drive	¾ to 2	1290	to	2100
"Saurer," International Motor Co., N. Y. City, 2 models. Chassis only. Chain drive	5 and 6½	4800	to	5800
"Schacht," The G. A. Schacht Motor Truck Co., Cincinnati, Ohio, 3 models. Bodies extra. Worm drive	1½ to 3	2650	to	3200
"Selden," Selden Truck Sales Co., Rochester, N. Y., 5 models. Bodies extra. Worm drive	¾ to 3½	985	to	3150
"Service," Service Motor Truck Co., Wabash, Ind., 5 models. Bodies extra. Worm drive	1 to 5	1375	to	4000
"Signal," Signal Motor Truck Co., Detroit, Mich., 5 models. Bodies extra. Worm drive	1 to 5	1550	to	4000
"Standard," Standard Motor Truck Co., Detroit, Mich., 3 models. Chain and Worm drive	2 to 5	2300	to	3700
"Stanley," Stanley Motor Carriage Co., Newton, Mass., 2 models, steam power. Bodies extra	¾ to 1¼	1775	to	2200
"Stegeman," Stegeman Motor Car Co., Milwaukee, Wis., 5 models, 6 cylinders. Bodies extra. Worm drive	2 to 7	2250 to 4600		

Make & Description	Tons	Price
"Sterling," Sterling Motor Truck Co., Milwaukee, Wis., 4 models. Chassis only. Worm and Chain drive	2½ to 7	2800 to 5250
"Stewart," Stewart Motor Corp., Buffalo, N. Y., 3 models. Bodies extra. Internal Gear drive	¾ to 1½	795 to 1485
"Studebaker," Studebaker Corp. of America, Detroit, Mich., 2 models. With and without bodies. Shaft drive	½ and 1	876 to 1250
"Superior," E. G. Willingham's Sons, Atlanta, Ga., 2 models. Bodies extra. Internal Gear drive	1 and 2	1350 and 1800
"Thomas," Thomas Auto Truck Co., Inc., New York City, 1 model. Bodies extra. Worm drive	2 to 2½	2700
"Ton A Ford" (Extension Chassis), Ton A Ford Truck Co., Racine, Wis. Ford chassis and motor. Bodies extra	1	685
"Tower," Tower Motor Truck Co., Greenville, Mich., 5 models. Bodies extra	¾ to 3	1150 to 2500
"Trabold," Trabold Truck Mfg. Co., Johnstown, Pa., 2 models. Chassis only	1 and 2	975 and 1750
"Trojan," The Commercial Truck Co., Cleveland, Ohio, 2 models. Bodies extra. Worm drive	1	1500 and 1600
"United," United Motors Co., Grand Rapids, Mich., 4 models. Bodies extra. Worm drive	2 to 5	2250 to 3900
"U. S.," United States Motor Truck Co., Cincinnati, Ohio, 5 models. Bodies extra. Chain and	2½ to 5	2500 to 4400

Worm drive

"Universal," Universal Service Co., Detroit, Mich., 4 models. Bodies extra. Chain and Worm drive	1½ to 3	2000 to	3400
"Veerac," Veerac Company, Minneapolis, Minn., 3 models, 2 cylinders. Complete. Chain drive	¾ and 1	950 to	1150
"Velle," Velle Motors Corp., Moline, Ill., 2 models. Bodies extra. Worm drive	2 and 3½	2250 and	3350
"Viall," Viall Motor Car Co., Chicago, Ill., 4 models. Chassis only. Chain and Worm drive	1½ to 5	1650 to	3250
"Vim," Vim Motor Truck Co., Philadelphia, Pa., 12 delivery bodies. Complete. Bevel Gear drive		695 to	1385
"Voltz," Voltz Brothers, Chicago, Ill., 2 models. Bodies extra. Chain drive	3 and 5	2750 and	3600
"Walter," Walter Motor Truck Co., N. Y. City., 6 models. Also tractor. Bodies extra. Internal Gear drive	3 to 7½	4000 to	4500
"Ware," Twin City Four Wheel Drive Co., St. Paul, Minn., 3 models. Complete. Direct Shaft drive	2½ and 5	2800 to	4800
"Watson," Watson Wagon Co., Canastota, N. Y. Tractor and Trailer	5	On application	
"White," The White Co., Cleveland, Ohio, 4 models. Bodies extra. Fire apparatus, etc., special. Chain and Shaft drive	¾ to 5	2100 to	4500

"Wichita," Wichita Falls Motor Co., Wichita Falls, Texas, 8 models. Bodies extra. Worm and Chain drive	1 to 5	1650 to	3850
"Wilcox Trux," Wilcox Motor Truck Co., Minneapolis, Minn., 5 models. Bodies extra. Worm drive	¾ to 3½	On application	
"Wilson," J. C. Wilson Co., Detroit, Mich., 4 models, 5-ton haulage. Body extra. Worm Gear drive	1 to 3	1375 to	2650
"Wisconsin," Myers Machine Co., Sheboygan, Wis., 4 models. Bodies extra. Worm drive	1¼ to 5	1650 to	4500
"Wonder," Wonder Motor Truck Co., Chicago, Ill., 1 model, 3 bodies. (Truck and Pleasure.)	1	800 to	850

ELECTRIC COMMERCIAL VEHICLES

"Atlantic," Atlantic Electric Vehicle Co., Newark, N. J., 4 models. With or without bodies. Chain drive	1 to 5	On application	
"Beardsley," Beardsley Electric Vehicle Co., Los Angeles, Cal., 2 models. Shaft drive	150 and 2000 lbs.	1185 and	2000
"C. T." Commercial Truck Co. of America, Phila., Pa., 5 models. Chassis only. Gear drive	½ to 5	1500 to	3500
"Couple Gear," Couple Gear Freight Wheel Co., Grand Rapids, Mich., 2 models. Four-wheel drive. Complete	3½ and 5	4400 and	5000
"Fritchie," Fritchie Electric Co., Denver, Colo., 1 model.	½	2000	

Complete

"G. V.," General Vehicle Co., Inc., Long Island City, N. Y., 6 models. Bodies extra. Worm and Chain drive	½ to 5	1700 to 3700	
"Lansden," Lansden Co., Inc., Brooklyn, N. Y., 6 models. Chassis only. Chain and direct drive	½ to 6	1460 to 3500	
"Mercury," The Mercury Mfg. Co., Chicago, Ill., 3 models	Tractor	1274 to 4435	
"Walker," Walker Vehicle Co., Chicago, Ill., 6 models. Chassis only. Tractors up to 10 tons. Balance drive	½ to 5	On application	
"Ward," Ward Motor Vehicle Co., Mount Vernon, N. Y., 5 models. Chassis only. Worm and Helical Bevel drive	⅓ to 5	760 up	